WHAT THE MAFIA CAN TEACH
THE LEGITIMATE BUSINESSMAN

Louis Ferrante

Portfolio / Penguin

PORTFOLIO / PENGUIN
Published by the Penguin Group
Penguin Group (USA) Inc., 375 Hudson Street,
New York, New York 10014, U.S.A.
Penguin Group (Canada), 90 Eglinton Avenue East, Suite 700,
Toronto, Ontario, Canada M4P 2Y3
(a division of Pearson Penguin Canada Inc.)
Penguin Books Ltd, 80 Strand, London WC2R 0RL, England
Penguin Ireland, 25 St Stephen's Green, Dublin 2, Ireland
(a division of Penguin Books Ltd)
Penguin Books Australia Ltd, 250 Camberwell Road, Camberwell,
Victoria 3124, Australia
(a division of Pearson Australia Group Pty Ltd)
Penguin Books India Pvt Ltd, 11 Community Centre, Panchsheel Park,
New Delhi – 110 017, India
Penguin Group (NZ), 67 Apollo Drive, Rosedale, Auckland 0632,
New Zealand (a division of Pearson New Zealand Ltd)
Penguin Books (South Africa) (Pty) Ltd, 24 Sturdee Avenue,
Rosebank, Johannesburg 2196, South Africa

Penguin Books Ltd, Registered Offices:
80 Strand, London WC2R 0RL, England

First published in 2011 by Portfolio / Penguin,
a member of Penguin Group (USA) Inc.

3   5   7   9   10   8   6   4   2

Library of Congress Cataloging-in-Publication Data

Ferrante, Louis.
Mob rules : what the Mafia can teach legitimate businessmen / Louis Ferrante.
p. cm.
Includes bibliographical references and index.
ISBN 978-1-59184-398-6
1. Strategic planning   2. Success in business.   3. Management.   4. Mafia.
5. Organized crime.   I. Title.
HD30.28.F474 2011
658.4'012—dc22
2010053098

Printed in the United States of America
Set in Granjon LT Std
Designed by Spring Hoteling

To Gabriella, and her mother, Angelika
—an angel on Earth, the other in Heaven

The organization chart of a crime family or syndicate mirrors the management structure of a corporation. At the top of the pyramid is a boss, or chief executive. Below him are an underboss (chief operating officer) and a consigliere (general counsel). Then follow ranks of capos (vice presidents) and soldiers (lower-level employees who carry out the bosses' orders). Like corporations, crime groups often rely on outside consultants.

—*Fortune* magazine

CONTENTS

Author's note   xvii

Preface   xix

Introduction   1

PART I
LESSONS FOR A SOLDIER (EMPLOYEE)

Lesson 1
Make Them an Offer They Can't Refuse:
A Surefire Way to Get Hired   9

Lesson 2
It's the Principle!:
When to Make a Point   11

Lesson 3
Why Are the Mobsters in the Newspapers So Old?:
Love What You Do and You'll Never Work a Day in Your Life   13

Lesson 4
Hide Your Gun and Help the Old Man Across the Street:
Family Values   17

Lesson 5
The Mob Doesn't Take Notes:
Sharpen Your Memory   19

Contents

Lesson 6
Don't End Up in the Trunk of a Car:
Avoiding Office Politics   21

Lesson 7
Three Can Keep a Secret if Two Are Dead: Trust   23

Lesson 8
Why Italians Cut Up Pigs and Cook
Them in the Sauce: Greed   25

Lesson 9
It's Good to Go to a Funeral as Long as It's Not Yours:
The Power of Networking   28

Lesson 10
Ole Blue Eyes: Why Mobsters Love Sinatra   32

Lesson 11
Turning Garbage into Gold:
Sniffing Out Opportunity   35

Lesson 12
Roll Up Your Sleeves but Keep Your Pants On   40

Lesson 13
The Walls Have Ears: Never Bad-Mouth the Boss   42

Lesson 14
Did You Wash Your Car or Screw It in the Muffler?:
Verbal Skills   45

Lesson 15
Count On Yourself and You'll Never Be Counted Out   47

Lesson 16
How Luciano Became Lucky:
Make Your Own Luck   49

Lesson 17
The Bank of Favors Pays the Highest Interest   52

Lesson 18
Why "The Chin" Wore Pajamas to Work:
When to Play Dumb   55

Contents

Lesson 19
The School of Hard Knocks: Experience   58

Lesson 20
Is This Phone Tapped?:
Watch What You Say Every Day   61

Lesson 21
He Should Kill Gus Farace or Kill Himself:
Respecting the Chain of Command   63

Lesson 22
Go Get Your Own Coffee!:
Respecting the Chain of Command Without Being a Sucker   66

Lesson 23
Kill or Be Killed: When to Defy Orders   69

Lesson 24
Plato—Didn't He Own a Swingers' Club?:
Be Informed   71

Lesson 25
I Want My Fucking Money:
Paying Promptly   73

Lesson 26
Don't Tip Your Hand:
When to Keep Quiet   74

Lesson 27
Capone, Harvard, and Yale:
The Key to Growth   76

Lesson 28
The Bug and the Jaguar: Patience   78

Lesson 29
Stick Your Handouts Up Your … :
Cultivate Aggressiveness   80

Lesson 30
Be the Master of Your Own Fate,
Not a Master of Disguises   82

Contents

PART II
LESSONS FOR A CAPO (MIDDLE MANAGEMENT)

Lesson 31
Bacon, Lettuce, and DeMeo:
You're Responsible for Your Crew   87

Lesson 32
How to Hit Your Target Without a Gun:
Motivating Your People   91

Lesson 33
Let's Meet in the Back for a Sit-down:
Mediating Disputes and the Art of Compromise   93

Lesson 34
When to Take a Bullet for the Boss   96

Lesson 35
Why Hit Men Tell Jokes over a Dead Body:
Bonding with Subordinates   97

Lesson 36
Nino Gaggi's Magic Bullet: The Mob Never Kills a Good Idea   99

Lesson 37
Toss the Dice High: Dealing with Unreasonable Ultimatums   103

Lesson 38
How to Bury the Hatchet—but Not in Someone's Head   105

Lesson 39
Take That Stone from My Shoe: Firing and Hiring   107

Lesson 40
The Toughest Guys Have the Thinnest Skin:
Never Embarrass Someone in Public   110

Lesson 41
The Mafia Isn't Turning Yellow, but Going Green:
Keeping Up with the World   111

Lesson 42
Flashiness Can End in the Flash of a Gun: Modesty   113

Contents

Lesson 43
Why a Mobster Makes His Son Pull the Trigger:
Confidence Building 116

Lesson 44
Seize the Bull by the Horns—and Rip Off Its Balls:
The Fast and Decisive Leader 118

Lesson 45
Just Get the Job Done!: Flexibility 121

Lesson 46
We Shot Him Twelve Times and He Lived:
Most Problems Take Care of Themselves 123

Lesson 47
Aye, You Know Who My Uncle Is?: Everyone Is Important 124

Lesson 48
What Am I, a Gavone?:
What People Really Think About You 128

Lesson 49
Play the Fence and You're Sure to Fall Off 130

Lesson 50
Italians Talk with Their Hands: Body Language 132

Lesson 51
Deliver the Goods: Stand Behind Your Name 134

Lesson 52
Fireproof Your Ass:
Never Let Anyone Light a Flame Under You 136

Lesson 53
Go to Bat for Your Guys: Loyalty to Your Employees 138

Lesson 54
Rest in Peace—in a Lakeside Cabin, Not an Early Grave:
Taking a Break and Coming Back Refreshed 140

Lesson 55
Don't Split Yourself in Half:
The Wrong Decision Is Better Than None at All 142

Contents

Lesson 56
New Orleans Wasn't Built in a Day   144

Lesson 57
Bugsy and Bacchus: The Lessons of History   146

Lesson 58
Time to Go: How to Leave the Organization   149

PART III
LESSONS FOR A DON (BOSS)

Lesson 59
You Gotta Know When to Fold 'em:
Controlling Your Ambition   153

Lesson 60
It's Strictly Business: Friends or Enemies?   156

Lesson 61
The Mafia Spends Very Little on Office Supplies:
Cutting Overhead   158

Lesson 62
Social Clubs Have Solid Steel Doors—That Are Always Open:
An Open-Door Policy   160

Lesson 63
Don't Bother Me Now!:
The Value of Interruptions   162

Lesson 64
The Bail Money's in the Bedside Drawer:
Get It Right Ahead of Time   164

Lesson 65
Don't Build Yankee Stadium, Just Supply the Concrete:
Spotting New Rackets   165

Lesson 66
Give the IRS Their Vig:
What We've Learned from Al Capone   167

Contents

Lesson 67
Victory Without Follow-up Is Like Pasta Without Dessert:
Crisis Management   169

Lesson 68
The Power of an Elite Circle:
Why the Mob Opens and Closes the Books   173

Lesson 69
Give the Spic Bastard a Call!: Hiring the Best Person,
Regardless of Race, Creed, or Sexual Orientation   175

Lesson 70
A Little Give and Take: Hospitality   178

Lesson 71
Tip the Coat Check: Charity   180

Lesson 72
Eat, Drink, and Be Productive:
The Only Bribe I'll Advise You to Make   184

Lesson 73
I'm Comin' on the Heist Tonight: The Hands-on Boss   187

Lesson 74
A Tough Guy Has Balls. A Smart Guy Has Crystal Balls:
Foresight   189

Lesson 75
Never Underestimate Your Opponent   191

Lesson 76
Who Is Your Opponent?   193

Lesson 77
Don't Shoot a Rising Star:
Neutralizing Potential Opponents   197

Lesson 78
They Can Take It in the Ass on My Dance Floor:
Don't Let Opinions Stand in the Way of Profit   199

Lesson 79
Choosing Your Consigliere   202

Contents

Lesson 80
Why Frankie Fever Don't Believe the Hype   203

Lesson 81
I Got an Inside Guy: Staying Up on the Competition   205

Lesson 82
Hide Your Money Under the Mattress: Stay Cash Heavy   206

Lesson 83
Poverty Sucks. Or Does It?   207

Lesson 84
The Mafia Is a Brand Name: When to Franchise   209

Lesson 85
It's Good to Be King: But No One Is Above the Law   210

Lesson 86
Guys Like Us, Guys Like Them:
Stick with What You Know   212

Lesson 87
Marcus Aurelius Was a Great Emperor,
but That Doesn't Mean His Son Was: The Perils of Nepotism 215

Lesson 88
Leave the Gun, Take the Cannolis... and Beware of Hubris 218

Epilogue
Be a Pizza Egg Roll   221

ACKNOWLEDGMENTS   223

NOTES   225

BIBLIOGRAPHY   233

INDEX   241

AUTHOR'S NOTE

Readers of my memoir, *Unlocked,* know that in that book I had changed the names of men I had committed crimes with in order to conceal their true identities. I have never snitched on fellow mobsters or anyone else, and although I chose to leave the Mafia while in prison, I remain true to my former associates. In this book, with few exceptions, I use actual names since the mobsters I write about are dead, in prison, or have cooperated with the government. Nothing I write here can lead to criminal indictments. I am not uncovering crimes or pointing out targets for law enforcement, but simply highlighting the acute business sense of the Mafia.

Throughout this book, I refer to organized crime as the Mob or the Mafia. These serve as accessible terms; however, they are seldom if ever used by members of a crime family who refer to their organizations as La Cosa Nostra, meaning "our thing," or the *borgata,* meaning "the family."

I apologize in advance for any colorful language.

PREFACE

IN ancient Sparta, boys around the age of twelve underwent a peculiar education designed to sharpen their wits and teach them the skills necessary to succeed in a harsh world. In the hills surrounding the militaristic city-state, the boys were underfed to the point of starvation, then sent into town to steal food in order to survive. They would have to be clever and cunning; if caught, they were severely punished. Not for stealing, but for failing.

The Spartans believed that a young man who could master the skills of a thief would flourish in life. I don't advise anyone to become a thief in an effort to excel, but by studying the underlying nature of successful criminals, one can glean many valuable lessons.

> A career of banditry in early youth often indicated a man of strong character and purpose.
> —Edgar Snow, **Red Star over China**

I began stealing at age twelve. I operated an automobile chop shop in my early teens, hijacked my first truck in my late teens, and was heading my own crew of much older men within the Gambino crime family by my early twenties. I was suspected of pulling off some of the largest heists in U.S. history before the age of twenty-one.

Without higher education, I relied on instincts to navigate the treacherous but profitable world of the Mafia, netting millions of dollars for my family, or company. At any given time, my life in the Mafia cast me in three separate roles. I was an employee for the Gambino family; I was the boss, or CEO, of my own crew; and I was middle management, taking orders from Mafia chieftains and handing them down to underlings. Thus, I'm well qualified to speak to individuals on each rung of the corporate ladder.

I was never caught committing a crime, but information from confidential informants resulted in several investigations.

After a highly prosperous run, I was taken down by state law enforcement officers and federal agents, who pieced together cases against me using these informants. I faced the rest of my life in prison, and was asked to cooperate against other mobsters in return for my freedom. I refused to inform on friends and associates, and my lawyers negotiated a plea bargain after the main snitch against me was thrown out of the government's Witness Protection Program. I was sentenced to twelve and a half years and sent to the maximum security penitentiary in Lewisburg, Pennsylvania.

In prison, I realized that crime was wrong. Sure, life is a struggle and we can't live it on our knees, but I didn't have the right to victimize people. I decided to change my life.

While in prison, I read my first book. It wasn't easy at first; my vocabulary sucked, as did my attention span and ability to grasp whatever I read. But I stuck with it and discovered the joy of reading. Soon, stacks of books lined the floor of my cell, were shoved under my bunk, and piled around the toilet. Where posters of nude women decorated the stone walls of other cons' cells, maps covered mine. For years, I read every day until the muscles in my eyes ached and I would conk out from sheer exhaustion. A few hours' sleep, long enough to rest my eyes, then back to the books. My cell became a live-in classroom where I studied every subject possible. I personally reversed one of my federal cases from prison and was released after serving eight and a half years. By then, I'd taught myself the art of writing by analyzing the novels of nineteenth-century masters and I had written a novel of my own.

Upon my release from prison, I had this glorious notion that I was leaving criminal behavior behind, and with it the variety of rogues I'd dealt with on a daily basis on the street. I dreamed of taking up my place in the legit world. How different it would be from the life I'd known.

To my surprise, I realized that my idea of the legit world was a fantasy. I soon encountered creeps in legal society far worse than many of the mobsters I'd known—these wolves all hid in sheep's clothing.

As a loan shark, I never increased the interest rate on someone's loan. If anything, I dropped the rate as a reward for timely payments. Credit card companies increase your rate, regardless of your history, and do so without your knowledgeable consent. How about all those hidden fees? "It's in the small print," one customer service rep told me. "You should have read it." That's like me increasing someone's vig on a loan, and saying to him, "When I gave you the money, I whispered that part. You should have heard me."

Collection agencies call a person's house and harass whoever answers the phone. They don't care if your mom or grandmother is about to drop dead. Too bad, pay up! Say what you want about the Mob, but Mafia code forbids mobsters to even go near a man's home, let alone harass his family.

Banks foreclose on homes and toss the occupants into the street. The local sheriff issues a court order, locks the door, and throws the family out. I'd bet any dad who lives through that would rather deal with us. You might get a couple of broken bones, maybe a black eye; big deal, you still own your home.

Let's be real: mobsters are selfish men, out for personal gain, but so are businessmen. Mobsters may kill their own, but everyone else gets a little slack. Most businessmen, banks, and credit card companies prey on everyone.

> We only kill each other.
>
> —Benjamin "Bugsy" Siegel

As a mobster, I was feared, so vultures stayed clear of me. As a legit guy, I became fair game; everyone tried to screw me.

Coming home from prison, I needed a car and an apartment.

Time and again, I was bullshitted by car salesmen with the old bait-and-switch. Every time I was ready to sign on the dotted line, the deal changed.

I rented an apartment. During the winter, my landlord wouldn't turn up the heat, but the cheap bastard wanted his rent on time. I had to buy an electric heater. When I left and asked for my security back, he hemmed and hawed, claimed he didn't have it.

I shopped for a house. Every mortgage broker tried to put me into an adjustable rate loan, which they swore would never go up. I knew they were lying. When I threatened to return with a baseball bat if it just so happened to go up, they promptly admitted that the rate could very well increase.

I can't count how many times I threw up my hands and said, "What a bunch of crooks!" I felt surrounded by predators, not unlike the streets, or worse, prison, where I had to watch my back every second.

I'm not the first to notice that prison is a lot like ordinary society. Jonathan Swift, eighteenth-century author of *Gulliver's Travels,* commented that convicts in prison, when it came to morals, weren't all that different from people in high society.

Speaking of Jonathan Swift, I felt like Gulliver, all tied up and stepped on by people much smaller than myself. It was time for me to stand up.

I decided to unlock the aggressive spirit I'd developed in the Mafia, a world in which I first had to survive before I could succeed.

> Whereas I, lost among the obscure crowd, have had
> to deploy more knowledge, more calculation and skill

merely to survive than has sufficed to rule all the provinces of Spain for a century!

—Figaro in Pierre Beaumarchais's *The Marriage of Figaro*

I suddenly had a great advantage over these small people; my life experiences were the training ground for success.

The life I'd lived, which I often regretted, was also the life that taught me how to defend against predators, sniff out a bullshitter, and outfox a snake. It was a life that taught me to be self-reliant, to think big, and to believe in myself.

In the Mafia, I learned to take the initiative, come up with a new idea, and put it into action. I learned how to communicate with people. To the satisfaction of both parties, I settled beefs between doctors, lawyers, bankers, and brokers, men with impressive academic credentials who lacked the basic ability to talk things out. Having dealt with many and varied people in my past, I could hobnob as easily in polite society as in the ghetto. I could bullshit with a bum or forge an alliance with a banker; I could speak with anyone.

I also developed a knack for eliminating obstacles. I sometimes pushed them aside; other times, I plowed straight through them.

There are now no Alps.

—Napoleon dismissing the largest obstacle on his road to conquering Italy
(Napoleon was born and raised on the island of Corsica, an island that revered its bandits; this native influence always remained a part of him. And he controlled France like a Mob boss.)

The Mafia often gets its way by strong-arming people. But more times than not, mobsters accomplish the same end by befriending someone, ingratiating themselves with that person, then simply asking for what they want.

After re-evaluating my idea of "legit" society, I found that my new clique was a lot like my old clique, less violent but sometimes more cunning. I continued to practice the civil aspects of Mafia life, ditched the rest, and success followed. The ancients would've been proud; I was a contemporary testament to the Spartan "Thief Theory."

Today I dedicate my life to helping people. My memoir, *Unlocked,* has reached readers all over the world, and I receive a constant flow of fan mail from people who tell me that my book has changed their lives. I've appeared on television in over two hundred countries and speak before various audiences, from hardened cons to probation officers, from youth groups to senior citizens, from colleges and universities to business organizations and library conferences.

Like the Homeric Greeks, Talmudic Jews, and Native American storytellers, older mobsters use the oral tradition to school their young and hand down the seasoned wisdom of the streets. Throughout this book, I continue the age-old tradition of storytelling to convey that wisdom. When appropriate, I supplement Mafia stories with historical anecdotes to emphasize that any lesson can be universally applied and that nothing changes under the sun. If you learn what happened yesterday, you'll be prepared for what's bound to happen tomorrow. I've also interspersed relevant quotes throughout the text to reinforce a point and encourage further reading.

This book is designed to teach the better attributes of La Cosa Nostra, so that Our Thing can become Your Thing.

INTRODUCTION

THE Mafia is the longest-running corporation in history. It thrives along with other companies during prosperous times and flourishes even more in periods of economic decline. Bear or bull makes no difference to the Mafia.

Al Capone's soup kitchens fed thousands every day during the Great Depression. Why was Al able to dish out all that soup? How were Bugsy Siegel and Meyer Lansky able to visualize a multibillion-dollar resort called Las Vegas when their more legitimate contemporaries saw only a sleepy little desert town? Why, at this moment of deep economic uncertainty, is the Mob thriving, scooping up real estate across the country while millions fight foreclosure?

The fact is, for all the Mob's well-deserved reputation for violence, its most successful members have always been remarkably astute businessmen, bringing to the table an uncommon brand of entrepreneurial acumen—even a set of strong values, born of their unique background.

> Mr. Persico . . . you are one of the most intelligent people I have ever seen in my life.
> —Judge John F. Keenan's comment on Don Carmine Persico's *pro se* courtroom performance

These individuals would have succeeded in any field they chose, and indeed many built their fortunes in ventures far removed from organized crime. They applied their street smarts to legal enterprise and earned millions doing so.

> His intelligence and personality might have served him well in legitimate business.
> —Judge Joanna Seybert's comment at the sentencing of Don Alphonse "Allie Boy" Persico, son and successor of Don Carmine Persico

Accustomed to a daily struggle for supremacy, mobsters are well prepared to triumph in any sphere and under any circumstances. Mobsters who have successfully crossed over into the straight world have done so by retaining their aggressive nature, but tempering it so as not to frighten people out of doing business with them entirely. Their typical bullying tactics are supplanted by rocklike firmness combined with charismatic persuasion. In short, they ditch the guns and daggers while dressing up their other Darwinian traits.

> Mafia families are cut from a special kind of human cloth: they include people of especially strong aggressive and predatory tendencies.
> —Pino Arlacchi, *Mafia Business*

Some mobsters I've known have gone legit but taken a bit longer to shed their Mafia skin. At the start, they bully and frighten off their competition, and force others into doing business with them— or else. It's tough to shake old habits. However, even for these men, legitimate success inevitably leads to a complete disavowal of criminal behavior. Why risk jail time when such a vast fortune is at stake? Why act like a hoodlum if you don't have to? Why build an empire and destroy it with fraud?

Many would think that even if a mobster refrains from using coercion in the business world, the threat is implied because of his background. Thus, not much has to be said or done to gain a foothold in a particular neighborhood, acquire a contract, or negotiate a sweetheart deal. True, some mobsters enjoy the benefits of their reputations. But just as many go to great lengths to conceal their underworld credentials.

For twenty years, no one in my neighborhood of Flushing, Queens, knew that the local Key Food supermarket was owned by a top mobster until newspapers leaked the story. In fact, Gambino capo Patsy Conte owned several supermarkets, and sat on the board of directors for the Key Food supermarket chain.

Conte never said, "Buy my food or else!" Instead, he sat in an office quietly figuring out whom to appoint to management, what products to sell the consumer, and where to source the freshest meat and produce at the lowest cost. Conte kept hundreds, if not thousands, of people employed. Not bad for a mobster, huh?

I could name a dozen large, successful companies off the top of my head that are owned or largely run by both active and former mobsters. For all appearances, the companies are legit; none endorse Mafia policies, yet they owe their prosperity to Mafia savvy, polished and honed for honest use.

Armed with only strong, likable personalities, mobsters have gained entry into plenty of surprising places.

> Some of them, except for the criminal part of their life, can be very nice people.
> —Former New York City mayor Rudolph Giuliani

The Mafia didn't shoot their way into Vatican City but oversaw the finances of the Catholic Church in 1971. Their profitable run came to an end only in 1978, after the suspicious death of a pope.

President Jimmy Carter unwittingly named reputed Gambino capo Anthony Scotto as a candidate for secretary of labor. Ronald Reagan's secretary of labor, Ray Donovan, was acquitted in a trial that linked him to New York's Genovese family. I'm not sure if Reagan realized how close to home his words were when he said, "Today, the power of organized crime reaches into every segment of our society."

How does a mobster, a mere street thug dressed in a suit with a splash of cologne, work his way into the Vatican or the White House or onto the board of a supermarket chain?

If we shed our prejudices, we'll find that successful mobsters are not unlike top business or political leaders. The Mafia shares the same power structure as any government or corporation, and the same savvy is needed to climb the ladder of all three organizations. Many key government posts are filled by corporate successes; their transitions into government are smooth because the essential qualities needed for success, once understood and attained, can be applied in any field.

Because human nature is constant, a person who acquires diplomatic skills and leadership qualities and can motivate others can succeed in any organization, whether government, corporate, or Mafia.

If you're a student of political science or business administration, or just eager to succeed, it's worth a look at the black sheep of this power trio: the Mafia.

> These criminal gangs have such power that they consti-
> tute a government within a government in this country.
> —Kefauver Committee hearings on organized crime,
> 1950–51

Colombo capo Thomas Petrizzo dropped out of school at sixteen. He failed at every business attempt he made into his forties. By then, he'd gained enough street smarts to succeed in any venture, eventually supplying steel for major construction projects and earning over $50 million a year. When Petrizzo was arrested on racketeering charges, his colleagues in the steel industry were astonished.

One of our nation's top steel executives said, "[Petrizzo] was one of the most sincere and honest people I ever met in this business; his services and word were like gold."

"His word is gold" is a key phrase used in the Mob whenever vouching for someone or passing on a verbal résumé. Whoever achieves this triple-A rating will inevitably meet with prosperity.

> My word is better than anything else I got to offer.
> —Salvatore Profaci, capo and son of Joe Profaci, founder of what would become known as the Colombo family

Petrizzo played a large part in constructing some of the biggest projects in New York: the World Financial Center, the IBM Building, South Street Seaport, and Battery Park City, to name a few.

In fact, every construction boom in New York has been spearheaded by Mafia-owned or -associated companies. The rapid growth of Manhattan's concrete skyline would have been seriously stunted without the Mob's contractors, earth-moving machinery, and smooth union leadership. In the 1980s, a study by New York State's Organized Crime Task Force concluded that our nation's top building developers preferred doing business with the Mafia over legitimate but mercurial union leaders.

> The success of the Mafia depends upon the excellence of its services; . . . [and] the loyalty of its millions of satisfied customers.
> —Nicholas Pileggi, *The Saturday Evening Post*

At every construction site in New York, a million little corruptions take place behind the dirt heap, each worthy of its own headline.

But above these whispers and the passing of envelopes, another sky-scraper rises in Manhattan. The capital of the world, home of the United Nations, and backdrop for the Statue of Liberty was built in large part by hardworking immigrants—under the secret leadership of La Cosa Nostra.

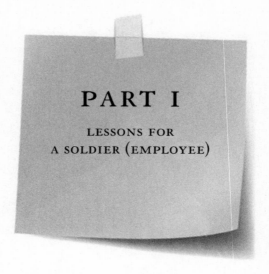

PART I

LESSONS FOR
A SOLDIER (EMPLOYEE)

Good morning, gentlemen, and anyone listening. This is the nine o'clock meeting of the Chicago underworld.

—Murray "The Camel" Humphreys,
general counsel for the Chicago Mafia

LESSON I

Make Them an Offer They Can't Refuse:
A Surefire Way to Get Hired

HOW does someone get in with the Mafia?

First, you have to want in, like any other potential employee who wants a job. In New York, it helps if someone in your immediate family belongs to one of the five crime families, like your dad or uncle. If so, chances are you'll end up in that particular family.

If your immediate family has no Mafia ties, and mine didn't, you're a cowboy, street guy, or free agent.

The Mafia has headhunters everywhere, just like corporations. If you're a street earner with a good name, a mobster from any one of the five families will find you. Once you're found, the mobster will put a "claim" on you. But the claim has mutual benefits. The mobster acquires a new source of income, while the street earner is invested with the collective power of the family, allowing him the potential to earn more than he ever did independently.

Unlike in the corporate world, once claimed, i.e. hired, you don't get a weekly paycheck, medical benefits, paid vacation, or sick days. You get shit, only a piece of what you earn.

What boss wouldn't hire a worker who expects to keep only a percentage of what he or she earns?

Tell any potential employer you don't want a paycheck, zilch, only a piece of what you earn, and you won't have to sit through many job interviews. Sure, some top companies might reject your offer if they're too selective, but a company that's hungry won't.

If you think this Mafia hiring method doesn't apply to the corporate world, you're wrong.

I once stood up for a rich Wall Street guy on a beef. After I straightened it out, he had his limo pick us up and drive us to Atlantic

City. On the way there, I asked him how he got his start on Wall Street.

He said that he started at a brokerage firm on Long Island. "I walked in off the street and asked for the manager," he explained. "All I wanted was a chance to prove myself. No set salary, just one month with a desk and a phone."

The manager was amused by his chutzpah and told him to start as a cold-caller since he hadn't yet taken the Series 7 exam qualifying him as a stockbroker. In that first month, his leads generated over ten thousand bucks in brokerage fees for the firm. Before his first year was up, he passed the broker's exam and became the company's top earner.

He exuded confidence, and the manager who hired him saw that self-confidence translating into profit.

> [Chris] Rosenberg was a small-time drug dealer but DeMeo liked his style. Chris was tenacious, cocky, and determined to make a sale.
>
> —*Mobsters: Roy DeMeo*

I laughed, and said to him, "We start out the same way in the Mob, strictly commission."

I once read that Warren Buffett, one of the world's richest men, started out just like us, offering his sweat for a small piece of what he earned for the company. Imagine hiring Warren Buffett for beans?

Confidence is an asset, something that doesn't show on a résumé. Make contact with people. Show your ambition. Let them know you're a go-getter. Everyone's looking for a good investment; that next investment should be you.

LESSON 2

It's the Principle!: When to Make a Point

THIS guy Alex owned a restaurant in Manhattan. He bet football and got in over his head with a bookie I knew.

Every night, Alex's restaurant was packed, reservations only, yet he continued to claim that he didn't have my friend's payments. So the bookie sent three bruisers to wreck his joint.

"I don't care if he offers you cash on the spot," the bookie told the bruisers before they left for the restaurant. "It's too late; it's now a question of principle."

Sure enough, Alex tried to square up with the three bruisers as soon as they walked in, just before closing time. Following my friend's orders, the bruisers refused Alex's cash and wrecked the place.

Alex eventually paid his debt. I asked my friend why he didn't accept the cash the night Alex had offered it. With hundreds of debtors, he explained to me, it was best to have a reputation as a businessman who stands on principle.

"If a bank never repossessed a car," he told me, "who would make a car payment?"

Most of us operate with a "take the money and run" attitude. How many of us are willing to stand on principle and accept a short-term loss to reap long-term benefits?

> We can't be letting these fucking assholes play us for fools. That gets around on the street, we're out of business.
>
> —Mobster Carmine Genovese

Don Salvatore Maranzano was one of the first American Mafia bosses. He studied the Roman Empire and structured his crime

11

family after the old Roman legions, with capos, or captains, assuming the role of legates, men who rule over a legion of soldiers. He even emulated Julius Caesar, establishing himself as emperor over his captains. Ironically, Maranzano was assassinated by his own men, just like his role model Caesar. But while in power, Maranzano stood firm on principle, also like Caesar.

Julius Caesar seized power in Rome after a bloody civil war against his arch-nemesis Pompey. After losing the war, Pompey sought refuge in Egypt. When Pompey arrived there, he was viciously murdered. The assassins then presented his head as a gift to Caesar.

You'd think Caesar would've been flattered by foreigners going to such lengths to please him, presenting him with the head of his enemy. Instead, Caesar promptly put Pompey's assassins to death. To Caesar, it was a question of principle. Although Pompey was his sworn enemy, he was still a Roman citizen, and no one had the right to take the life of a Roman citizen except the Roman government, i.e. Caesar. Had Caesar condoned the murder of a Roman citizen, where would it end?

The Mafia, like Caesar, avenges the unsanctioned death of a member, even if that member was hated and had it coming. Because of this, very few members have been murdered without a boss's permission.

The Mafia will stand on principle (when it's practical) for the sake of long-term profit, and simple survival.

LESSON 3

Why Are the Mobsters in the Newspapers So Old?:
Love What You Do and You'll Never
Work a Day in Your Life

THERE'S no such thing as a nine-to-five wiseguy. All those old mobsters photographed in the newspapers could have retired years before those embarrassing mug shots were taken, but they loved what they did and couldn't stop.

Louisiana boss Carlos Marcello and Chicago boss Anthony Accardo each had millions stashed away, enough to live wealthy for a hundred lifetimes, yet both were well into their eighties and still entrenched in The Life.

Bonanno boss Joe Massino was a multimillionaire. While on the lam in Pennsylvania, he walked into a pharmacy and boosted a bottle of aspirin. This small caper led to his arrest, a bigger headache than the one he needed the aspirin for. Why would a man worth millions, with bags of cash delivered to him every day, steal a measly bottle of aspirin? Because that's what Joe did. And he loved it.

> The thing you've got to understand about Jimmy [Burke] is that he loved to steal. He ate and breathed it. I think if you ever offered Jimmy a billion dollars not to steal, he'd turn you down and then try to figure out how to steal it from you. It was the only thing he enjoyed. It kept him alive.
>
> —Henry Hill, quoted in Nicholas Pileggi's *Wiseguy*

Sammy "The Bull" Gravano was worth over ten mil. Although he murdered more people than I can invite to a wedding, the government let him skate and keep the bulk of his dirty fortune in exchange for informing on his associates. Gravano was praised as an American hero by judges, prosecutors, and law enforcement officers, all of whom got a little bump in their careers after he helped them convict other mobsters. After getting a second chance at freedom, Gravano started up an international drug ring, embarrassing everyone who had called him a hero.

Gravano betrayed all his old friends; it's hard to believe his new government friends didn't expect this. He also loved what he did—crime—and returned to it the first chance he got.

Acting boss Anthony "Gaspipe" Casso caused a rift in the Lucchese family that nearly turned into a civil war. During the friction, a wiseguy I'll refer to as "Jake" was called in to see Gaspipe.

Jake was pretty certain Gaspipe was planning to kill him, and told me so.

"Why go if you think he'll kill you?" I asked.

Jake looked at me incredulously.

"I love this life," he said. "Enough to die for it."

> I'm going to a meeting and I don't know if I'm coming back.
> —Capo Dominick "Sonny Black" Napolitano speaks to a friend before being murdered

Can you imagine loving your job this much? Many people in all walks of life do.

Don Vincent "The Chin" Gigante loved his job so much that he let his capos keep most of the family profits. He'd get irritated with other bosses whenever a high-echelon meeting was called to discuss money. Gigante felt that family bosses should meet to keep peace, dictate policy, or enforce rules, not count dollars.

I personally loved being a mobster. It drove my whole being. Today, I love being a writer even more, a job where I can read and write every waking hour. Force me to do something I don't like and I'm a lazy son of a bitch.

If you find yourself voluntarily working after hours without being paid, you've found something you love to do. Until then, keep searching. Not everyone can love what they do. There are lots of boring jobs in this world, but the people who are content to fill them aren't reading this book.

Few people are fortunate enough to connect what they love with what they do. Don't settle and you'll be one of them.

If you've ever read about Carthage and its most famous general, Hannibal, you'll know that he ran his army like a Mob boss: unconditional rule, death to informants, steal as you go.

Carthage made war on Rome.

On his way to Rome, via Spain, Hannibal had a tough time crossing the Alps. Besides crappy weather, he met with fierce resistance; Alpine tribes formed hit teams and knocked off his soldiers left and right.

Hannibal grew disgusted; the Alpine assassins were darn good.

Then one day, a snitch gave Hannibal a tip. He told Hannibal that the tribal warriors who attacked his men by day went home each night, ate like gavones, fucked around with their wives, and fell asleep drunk.

Once Hannibal realized the hit squads were nine-to-five guys, he knew he had them beat. They were no match for Hannibal, who loved what he did; that's why he was freezing his ass off in the Alps.

The next night, after the hit teams punched their time cards and scurried home, Hannibal took the heights with his troops.

Early the next morning, those forty-hour-per-week warriors showed up at work and got the shit beat out of them. Hannibal broke through the mountain pass and was poised to conquer Rome.

Now the Romans broke their asses, too, and loved what they did, so Hannibal was in for a fight. But Hannibal and Rome changed the world and made history, while the lazy Alpine tribes have faded into oblivion. Who would you rather be?

LESSON 4

Hide Your Gun and Help the Old Man
Across the Street: Family Values

IT was a sunny afternoon. Four men, including myself, were sitting in a car with automatic weapons. We were staked out across the street from a trucking company, waiting for a truck to pull out of a warehouse so we could hijack it a few blocks away.

Suddenly, an old man stepped off the opposite sidewalk and began crossing the street toward us. He was not a very fast walker, and traffic was soon coming at him from both directions. He must've gotten dizzy; he started to wobble on his feet and then fell. All four of us dropped our guns and sprang from the car, racing toward him while waving off oncoming vehicles. We carried the old man to the curb, where he recovered. After a few minutes, we helped him to his feet and sent him on his way.

By this time, a small crowd had gathered around us. Now that we had all been seen by potential witnesses, the heist was off. We got back in our car and went to lunch.

We cursed the old man's timing, but none of us regretted helping him. There'd be other trucks to steal, but that poor old guy had only one life to live. I'm not saying we were angels—maybe fallen angels—since we were about to point a gun at somebody's head. But as bad as we were, we were taught at home, and in the Mafia, to respect our elders.

That's why all four of us were on the same page, willing to give up a million-dollar score to help an old man. Every wiseguy we told the story to that day joked and laughed, but agreed with our actions.

> But tell me, Charlie, why did you make that terrible mistake and go with Giuseppe? He's not your kind. He has no sense of values.
>
> —Salvatore Maranzano speaking
> to Charles "Lucky" Luciano

For all its savage brutality, the Mob has a sense of values. In fact, looking back, I have to credit the Mafia for some of my better attributes. The list of what I learned is long: be straightforward, don't give your word unless you can keep it, paying debts is just as important as collecting them, respect people's homes, don't hold a grudge . . .

In the Mob, the men who embrace the organization's values are those who go on to become the biggest earners.

Every company should have a set of values, and every employee should share those values. This common ground will be reflected in its image and business practices.

If dedication to a set of values, however twisted, produces success in a criminal society like the Mafia, how much further will genuine values propel you and your company in the straight world?

> Soldier: "My business is just buying and selling."
> Capo: "I don't want you selling that shit."
> Soldier: "But there's a lot of money in this. It's the way the industry is going. We can't stay competitive if we don't deal in it."
> Capo: "If you don't stop, you're gonna die."
> —Gambino capo demands that an underling involved in
> the porn industry stay away from
> child porn and bestiality, or pay with his life.

LESSON 5

The Mob Doesn't Take Notes:
Sharpen Your Memory

IN the movie *Goodfellas,* actor Paul Sorvino's character is based on Paul Vario, a legendary capo in the Lucchese family. On the street, I was introduced to Vario's grandson. I'll call him Bruno. Before we parted company, Bruno said to me, "Give me your number."

"Let me get a pen," I said, reaching into my car.

"No," said Bruno, "just tell me."

I reeled off my number. Bruno paused as if to make a mental note.

I was impressed. I was even more impressed when he called.

My friend Fat George DiBello was the caretaker of John Gotti's social club in Queens. George is a walking Rolodex. To this day, I can name any person from the old days and George will tell me the guy's birthday, marriage date, phone number, anything. Even the day and hour he died if he's no longer with us.

George may have been born with a sharp memory, but he honed his skills working at the club. In the criminal world, the less info that needs to be recorded, the better, in order to avoid incriminating paper trails.

> Trust your memory. Keep your business in your hat.
> —Meyer Lansky, the Mafia's Albert Einstein

Every day, mobsters use mnemonics, a formula that assists memory. Few, if any, know what the word *mnemonics* means, but they're experts at doing it. With hundreds of people in the Mob, it's difficult to remember everyone's name, so nicknames are given to aid memory: Johnny Blue Eyes. Greg the Nose. Paulie Pools. This is mnemonics.

How else can one mobster remember a small phone book of people in his head?

> It would have been difficult doing what Tony [Spilotro] did if he had secretaries, a filing system, Xerox machines, and the free use of a phone. But Tony did it all off-the-cuff and kept it all in his head.
>
> —Nicholas Pileggi, *Casino*

Joe Massino, former boss of the Bonanno family, ran a billion-dollar organization without pen, paper, or laptop—nothing. He knew every man in his army of soldiers, and every law enforcement agent who ever tailed him. If an agent questioned Massino and returned to question him years later, Massino remembered that agent's name and asked when the agent had switched cars, mentioning the make and model of the old car, including the license plate number.

Massino wasn't the only boss with a sharp memory.

I once had a sit-down with acting Lucchese boss Joseph "Little Joe" DeFede.

Our beef was probably one of a thousand DeFede presided over during his long career on the street. He and I spent less than an hour together, yet many years later, in prison, DeFede walked up to me and said, "Hi Louie, how ya been?"

Unfortunately for DeFede's crew, his outstanding memory made him an outstanding witness for the prosecution when the time got to him and he decided to flip.

Whether DeFede's memory was used to benefit the Mob or help dismantle it, it's further proof that a mobster's memory is sharp from years of relying on the mind to record important information.

> A large mass of recent evidence shows that memory ability is acquired, and it can be acquired by pretty much anyone.
>
> —Geoff Colvin, *Talent Is Overrated*

LESSON 6

Don't End Up in the Trunk of a Car:
Avoiding Office Politics

GAMBINO capo Artie the Hair-Do was on vacation with me at a horse ranch in upstate New York. One night, Sammy "The Bull" Gravano's name came up at the dinner table; he'd just been appointed underboss of our family. I hadn't yet met Sammy, so I asked Artie whether he liked him or not.

Artie looked at me, paused, then continued to eat. If Artie had cursed Sammy up and down, the impact wouldn't have been as profound as his silence. From that moment on, I knew to stay away from Sammy the Bull, who murdered some of his closest friends and relatives, and betrayed others when he went on to cooperate with the government. What I really learned from Artie was to keep my mouth shut when it came to office politics. After a half century of life on the street, Artie died of natural causes. Knowing when to be silent was, in part, the reason why.

> War is a very rough game, but I think that politics is worse.
> —Field Marshal Bernard Law Montgomery

Joe Bilotti was a tough old wiseguy built like an olive-skinned fire hydrant. Joe's brother was Tommy Bilotti, the underboss who got whacked along with Gambino boss Paul Castellano in front of Sparks Steak House in Manhattan.

When John Gotti succeeded Castellano as the new don of the family, he tossed around the idea of killing Joe too, concerned that Joe would avenge his brother's death. Joe, however, kept his mouth shut. He was smart enough to know that he didn't have the muscle to challenge Gotti. When questioned about his feelings, Joe shrugged and claimed he had none—strictly business.

You can say what you want about John Gotti's bloody reign, but any other tyrant, like Stalin or Mao, would have taken no chances. Joe would have been mincemeat. Colombian cartel leaders would even have wiped out Joe and Tommy's children, eighteen in all, to destroy any chance of a child growing up to avenge his father.

Although Gotti displayed mercy, Joe deserves the credit for his own survival; had he opened his mouth, he'd have been dead.

At the same time Joe Bilotti's life was being spared, another Gambino mobster, Louie Milito, was digging his own grave.

Milito had issues with the new regime's appointment decisions. He felt he was being pushed aside as promotions went to less experienced mobsters. Instead of holding his tongue like Bilotti, Milito expressed his dissatisfaction. The new regime called for his immediate dismissal. Milito's assassin put a bullet under his chin, a "shut the fuck up" shot.

> Louie [Milito] knew the rules . . . He played a very dangerous game—and he lost.
> —Sammy "The Bull" Gravano

Mobsters love the ponies, but they know the odds of losing at the track are far greater than those of winning. Getting involved in office politics is like betting the ponies—odds are you'll lose. The guy who stays ahead is the guy who watches the races but doesn't bet.

Artie the Hair-Do and Joe Bilotti knew when to keep quiet. Louie Milito's constant whispering was stopped by the whisper of a bullet passing through a silencer.

Avoid office politics. Your corporate survival is at stake.

LESSON 7

Three Can Keep a Secret if Two Are Dead: Trust

THE following sign hung above the door leading out of Louisiana Mob boss Carlos Marcello's office:

THREE CAN KEEP A SECRET IF TWO ARE DEAD

Marcello wanted everyone who'd just spoken with him to remember the importance of trust.

Growing up, I was friendly with Jesse Burke, son of Mafia heist man Jimmy Burke, the basis for Robert De Niro's character Jimmy Conway in the hit movie *Goodfellas*.

Jimmy Burke's fascination with outlaws was evident from the names he gave his two sons, Jesse James and Frank James, the pair named after the notorious James gang outlaws who held up banks and trains in the late 1800s.

Like the original Jesse James, Jimmy Burke gained his own notoriety when he pulled off the infamous Lufthansa heist.

Although the entire world now knows that Burke was the mastermind behind the heist, the crime remains officially unsolved to this day.

This is because Burke, unable to trust the men he did the heist with, killed nearly every one of them.

Plenty of mobsters have killed to keep a secret. That's why a smart mafioso holds on to someone who proves trustworthy, sometimes overlooking a shitload of other faults.

> I've never broken my word to any living human being I
> gave it to. That is the key to success in politics or any-
> thing else.
>> —Tom Pendergast, known as "Boss Tom," whose
>> Mafia-connected political dynasty was known as
>> "The Pendergast Machine"

I had a guy in my crew who was as dumb as Forrest Gump. Once, while on a heist, I told him to listen to the radio so he could warn us if cops were on the way. After the heist, I returned to the car to find him singing along to rock music, tapping his fingers on the steering wheel.

"What the fuck are you doing?" I asked, throwing the money bags into the car before sliding in. He lowered the volume.

"You told me to listen to the radio."

"The police scanner, you idiot!"

I had to laugh. He'd followed my orders literally. I trusted him and he was worth his weight in gold. In the future, I gave him explicit instructions; if he failed me, it was my own fault.

If you've done something to garner someone's distrust, you may already be written off. If you intend to be trusted in the future and can prove your worthiness over time, an apology certainly doesn't hurt.

If you're already a trustworthy person, realize you're a hot commodity. Don't offer your loyalty to just anyone. The wrong person or company will use or abuse you.

Numerous mobsters swore allegiance to Sammy "The Bull" Gravano. After the Castellano hit, the Bull said, "We made an agreement that nobody involved in this from here on out would ever speak to each other about it at any time under any circumstances and wouldn't admit anything to anybody else."

The Bull(shitter) then told this secret to prosecutors, judges, and anyone else who would listen; he even published it in a book that sold all over the world.

Be trustworthy. But be careful to whom you swear loyalty.

LESSON 8

Why Italians Cut Up Pigs and Cook Them in the Sauce: Greed

ON the afternoon of July 12, 1979, aspiring Bonanno don Carmine Galante sat down for lunch in a Brooklyn restaurant with four of his associates. As they finished their meal, three masked men rushed in, blasting away with automatic weapons. When the gunmen left, Galante and two of his companions were dead. The other two men at the table were unscathed.

Lucky guys? Not quite. The fix was in. Galante's own men had turned against him.

After the hit, the *New York Post* ran a gruesome photo of the slain Galante under the headline "GREED."

> I told you I'd get you. Greed got you killed.
> —Chicago hit man Sam DeStefano to Leo Foreman
> before killing him

Galante's leadership had been lacking in a number of areas, but the *Post* pinpointed the major source of discontent among Galante's fellow mobsters.

When Galante was murdered, the Bonannos were the only New York family that allowed their members to openly traffic in drugs. The other families also did it, but secretly. At the time of his death, Galante was attempting to shake down the Zips, or Sicilian-American mobsters, by demanding a street tax from the heroin market they controlled.

Galante's attempt to lord it over the Zips was dangerous. Even more dangerous than pissing off the Zips, Galante wasn't willing to split the take with the other New York families. An alliance with the other families might have given Galante the power he needed to control the Zips.

The Commission was convened, the order passed, and the execution carried out. Galante died biting down on a fat cigar, appropriate for a man who bit off more than he could chew.

> [Paul Castellano] is a greedy cocksucker. He wants the lion share of everything . . . the guy's never happy.
> —Anthony "Gaspipe" Casso

In the Mob, greed is prevalent at every level. Criminals are greedy by nature, so the share-out is usually a problem. The street guy with enough brains to overcome greed and distribute profits will rise quickly and safely.

The most successful mobsters aren't greedy. An old-timer once told me he'd been collecting fifty bucks a week from the same person for twenty years.

"To date," he said, "I've collected over fifty grand from the guy, and he never felt one payment. On top of that, he considers me his friend."

In business, resisting greed can benefit you in countless ways, including knowing when to get out of a stock, cash in your bonds, or avoid deals that are too good to be true.

Many of Bernie Madoff's investors were victims, blind to his bullshit. Some just covered their eyes. That's also greed. Beware of it in any form.

For a long time, the Mob ran the U.S. meat packing industry. Through Mafia suppliers, meat was trucked to major supermarket chains; one such supplier was a company named Merkel Meat.

The law caught the head of Merkel on tape, giving his recipe:

"On the patties, we got eighty pounds of cow meat and twenty pounds of filler. On the frankfurters, about 75 percent meat . . ."

We've all heard stories about franks being made from low-grade beef, but in Merkel's case, the filler was horse meat. It's not good when your grandmother pulls a meatloaf out of the oven that once ran in the Kentucky Derby.

Fortunately, we're not a starving nation; this was sheer greed.

But if you think mobsters are greedier than corporate execs, you're dead wrong. The Mob may have duped the American people with a little horse meat, but legit businessmen have the potential to do far more harm than the Mob.

During the Holocaust, German businesses competed for contracts to build equipment to murder and dispose of an entire segment of Europe's population.

One firm engineered a hot-tank to make soap. The instructions for best results called for "twelve pounds of human fat, ten quarts of water, and a pound of caustic soda . . . all boiled for two or three hours then cooled."

That makes Merkel look like a bunch of nuns.

Another German firm that acquired a contract wrote:

"For putting bodies into the furnace, we suggest simply a metal fork moving on cylinders. For transporting the corpses from the storage points to the furnaces we suggest using light carts on wheels, and we enclose diagrams of these drawn to scale."

The above-mentioned firms were staffed not by ideological Nazis but by greedy business execs.

As part of a major corporation or business, keep in mind you have the ability to do far more good in one day than the Mafia can ever do. And far more evil.

The future is in your hands. Beware of greed.

LESSON 9

It's Good to Go to a Funeral as Long as It's Not Yours: The Power of Networking

IN the early nineties, I was approached by Fritzi, a legit guy who heard I loaned out cash on the street. Fritzi wanted to open a gourmet deli in a hot spot near a university. Fritzi had found a good lease on a storefront, then arranged to get the snack racks and coolers on the arm from companies who supplied meat, soda, chips, and the like.

What Fritzi needed from me was cash; three months' security for the lease and money for renovations. In return, he offered me an equal partnership in the deli. I accepted.

I gave Fritzi the cash for the lease and introduced him to a carpenter I knew. The carpenter was a part-time thief who robbed materials from job sites, so he only charged us for his labor. Fritzi secured the lease with the landlord and began renovations.

While the deli was under construction, I stopped by to visit the carpenter. He told me that Fritzi was a major ball buster, adding that the only reason he hadn't already split his head open with the claw of a hammer was me.

I told the carpenter I'd talk to Fritzi. Before I left the deli, he asked me if the basement was part of our lease. I assumed it was and said so.

"It would make a great casino," he told me. "It's got a back entrance with a parking lot."

I checked out the basement. It was spacious, with high ceilings. It just needed a coat of paint, carpeting, and a dehumidifier. Behind the deli, there was a narrow driveway leading from the street to a parking lot that could hold a dozen cars.

I realized the carpenter was right—the place would make a great casino. I'd operate from ten P.M. till four A.M. when the rest of the stores on the block were closed. I left the deli feeling like Steve Wynn, the developer who made Las Vegas what it is today.

When I met with Fritzi that night, I asked him to ease up on the carpenter, particularly because the guy was prone to hammering objects other than nails. Fritzi got the picture immediately. Then I offered him an equal partnership in the basement casino. This was only fair since we were partners on the lease.

"I'll finish the basement, buy tables, hire dealers, and attract gamblers, but we'll split the profits down the middle, fifty-fifty."

As I said this, I could see the dollar signs flash in Fritzi's eyes like a cartoon cash register. Of course, he agreed. In no time at all, the renovations were completed.

About a week before the grand opening of our deli and casino, Fritzi phoned me.

"Meet me by the deli!" he told me. "We gotta talk!" *Told* me. Not *asked* me.

I figured this was a power move. Fritzi wanted to assert himself before we opened, figuring that a lot of cash would flow through the place and worried I might take advantage of him. Pretty sure this was the case, I planned to put his mind at ease, assuring him I'd never shortchange him, squeeze him out of the casino—or kill him.

I arrived at our little MGM Grand, parked my car, and went inside. Fritzi was standing in front of the deli counter with his head high and his arms folded across his chest, like a tough guy. But a fake tough guy. I laughed to myself, now certain he was afraid. Why else would he put up a front?

Fritzi surprised me. "I'm giving your money back. Thanks for lending it to me."

"What the fuck are you talkin' about?"

"I borrowed the money, now I'm paying you back. End of story."

"Whose voice is that?" I asked, assuming somebody gassed him up, looking to move in on the casino.

"Nobody," he said. "I speak for myself."

Normally, if involved in a beef on the street, it's mandatory for the guy you're beefing with to tell you who he answers to so you can arrange a sit and settle it diplomatically. Since Fritzi didn't defer to a higher power, I had a free hand to deal with him as I saw fit. If someone was pumping him up, there's one sure way to lure the puppet master out from behind the curtain: crush his puppet. I hit Fritzi with a right to the jaw and proceeded to beat his brains in.

We were about to open for business when this moron, blinded by dollar signs, decided he wanted everything for himself. Greed ruins everything.

When I left the deli, I put the incident "on record" with my own guy in the event someone emerged to defend Fritzi and the beef went to a sit. Later that evening, when I approached my house, I spotted an unmarked cop car parked across the street. I whipped a turn and sped away unnoticed. Apparently, Mr. Tough Guy had gone to the police.

I took it on the lam. From a cabin in the Poconos, I started to reach out to people. I needed to find someone Fritzi not only knew, but would listen to, in order to get the cops off my back.

Through the Mafia's large network of relations, my crew located that someone.

> Jimmy lived in a ritzy apartment in midtown. In his office, he had a big oak desk. In the top drawer was a sheet of paper taped to a piece of cardboard and covered in cellophane. It was a list of nicknames, across from each was a phone number. Every load I brought Jimmy went to someone on this list.
>
> —Louis Ferrante, *Unlocked*

Fritzi's father-in-law was a degenerate gambler—probably would've been a regular at our casino—and the father-in-law's bookie was a connected guy. My crew approached the bookie and asked him to do us a favor. The bookie told the father-in-law to have Fritzi call off the bulls or become olive loaf.

Fritzi came to his senses and dropped the charges. He sold the deli and paid me back my money with interest. And that was that.

The Mob has several thousand members and associates, and every one of them has his own network of crooked and legit friends. Every day, I used the Mafia's extensive network to earn money and, sometimes, as you've just seen, to save my freedom.

> OC [organized crime] has become a series of networks, a
> set of alliances, often across national boundaries.
> —Mike La Sorte, "Defining Organized Crime"

The Mafia was a MySpace community long before social networks sprang up all over the Web, but even the most impressive Mafia network is meager compared with Facebook and Twitter. To put today's networking possibilities in Mafia terms, you simply log on and you're a "made member" of the largest communities in the world. You can even consider yourself a "button man," the term used for a Mafia soldier, because you simply press a button and you're "connected."

Realize the extraordinary significance of networking, one of the most important elements of the Mafia's success.

LESSON 10

Ole Blue Eyes: Why Mobsters Love Sinatra

SICILY has always been clannish. Frank Sinatra's family came from the same Sicilian village as "Lucky" Luciano's family. This automatically qualified Frank as a goombah.

> The fact of having a common origin strengthens their bond, it makes them a tighter group.
> —Salvatore Lupo, *La Storia della Mafia*

Luciano booked a lot of singing gigs for Frank, and the Mob's control of nightclubs, jukeboxes, and music distribution also helped Frank early in his career.

In 1947, when the Mafia held a conference in Havana, Cuba, they took Frank along as a showpiece, for public relations. When later questioned by the FBI about the conference, Frank was tight-lipped. Being a stand-up guy further qualified Frank as a goombah in the Mafia's eyes. All told, Frank was loved by mobsters.

Today, Frank is dead, but the love affair continues. In part, mobsters are proud of Frank's Italian heritage; it boosts their pride. But more important, Frank's hard-luck lyrics touch their hearts. Quitting is our only true enemy in life, and Frank sang about never giving in.

Robert "Bobby Cabert" Bisaccia was a capo in the Gambino family who loved Frank Sinatra. Bobby had a murder conviction that would never get overturned due to incontestable evidence. He was serving a life sentence but slugged away at the law every day, trying to reverse his case.

One day, Bobby received a letter in the mail. It went something like this: "We are a prestigious law firm who has chosen to represent you pro bono. . . . We researched your case and are confident you will be a free man before Christmas."

The letter went on in this same hopeful tone. Bobby read it aloud for his fellow cons to its conclusion: "Until you hear anything further from us, continue with your escape plans."

Bobby let out a string of curses as the cons on his tier block, all in on the prank, burst out laughing. Bobby's refusal to quit fighting amused his fellow cons, who'd arranged to have the letter sent to him.

I met Bobby in federal prison when he was pulled over from Jersey State Prison to answer more murder charges. At the time, I was facing 125 years. Every morning, Bobby would say, "Answer the bell, kid."

It's fight talk. A boxer, regardless of how badly he's been beaten, must come out of his corner swinging when he hears the bell to start the next round.

Mobsters are natural-born sluggers, that's why so many have tried their luck in the ring.

I've been in the late Vincent "The Chin" Gigante's home office, where a painting of young Vincent as a boxer hung on the wall. He was a professional fighter before he dedicated himself to The Life and went on to become a don.

Even in that early painting, The Chin has a look of determination in his eyes. "I'm gonna be somebody," he seems to say.

Tommy Eboli, Anthony "Ham" Delasco, and "Machine Gun" Jack McGurn were other mobsters who, like Gigante, tried their luck in the ring before throwing in with the Mob.

An old friend I'll call Eddie has been linked to the Mob his whole career. Eddie told me a story that happened in the 1960s. While stationed down south in the army, he and his pals visited a local carnival. One of the carnival attractions offered a cash prize to any man who could slug it out with a baboon.

Eddie had the balls to get in the cage with the primate. He laughed as the cage door closed behind him, figuring the animal was only ninety pounds and winning the prize should be a cinch. He didn't realize the baboon's superhuman strength until the beast slapped the shit out of him and tried to mount him from behind.

With his face pressed against the cage, Eddie pleaded with his friends to shoot the beast. Fortunately for Eddie, the animal trainer was able to restrain the baboon before Eddie lost his virginity.

Eddie made it out of the cage, and the army. He went on to become a local boxing hero. In and out of the ring, Eddie has had more ups and downs than anyone around—but keeps fighting.

My life on the streets conditioned me to overcome failure. "Easy money" wasn't always so easy. I cracked open three safes before I found one with cash. I hijacked empty trucks, and dumped them on the side of the road. But the next day, I hijacked another.

I eventually pulled off big heists, but in the end I went to prison. There's no place in the world that can make you feel like a bigger failure than a prison cell. But I was conditioned not to quit.

How, though, can one succeed at anything in jail?

In prison, I picked up my first book, and was soon reading twenty hours a day. I taught myself the art of writing by studying how other authors wrote. I made prison, the asshole of the world, into my university—because every morning I answered the bell, like Bobby had told me. And I never gave in, like Sinatra sang.

That's why mobsters love Sinatra: he sang from the heart, a heart that wouldn't quit.

> I thought of quitting baby,
> But my heart just ain't gonna buy it.
> —Frank Sinatra, "That's Life"

LESSON II

Turning Garbage into Gold: Sniffing Out Opportunity

IN the 1930s, following a string of organized crime convictions, New York prosecutor Thomas Dewey claimed the Mafia was dead. He was wrong. The Mob was alive and well, but Dewey thought the claim might help him get into the Oval Office. He was wrong about that, too.

In the 1990s, after convicting the heads of the New York crime families, prosecutor Rudolph Giuliani also claimed the Mafia was dead. Like Dewey, Giuliani was wrong. The Mafia was alive and well, but Giuliani thought the claim might get him into the Oval Office. Like Dewey, he was wrong about that, too.

> Eradication of organized crime is pure fantasy.
> —Frederick Martens, chief of organized crime intel-
> ligence, New Jersey State Police

To become president of the United States, a politician must convince the voters he will "give the people what they want."

Apparently, neither Dewey nor Giuliani were able to convince the majority of American voters that they would give them what they wanted, while the Mafia has been doing just that since its inception: giving people what they want, and also what they need.

> I am just a businessman, giving the people what they want.
> —Al Capone

Fictional character Tony Soprano had a no-show job as a consultant for a waste management company; countless real-life mobsters have made billions of dollars disposing of trash.

On Long Island, New York, Lucchese capo Salvatore Avellino

disposed of garbage so well that local governments allowed Sal and his friends to literally do their dirty work for decades, aware that they themselves could not have done it better.

By the time the feds put the squeeze on Avellino, he'd collected enough garbage to fill the Meteor Crater in Arizona.

Sir Isaac Newton, the great British scientist credited with discovering gravity, wasted a shitload of time trying to turn cheap metals into gold, a practice called alchemy. Although alchemy didn't work, the Mob pays homage to Newton every day by turning garbage into gold.

The Mafia and Newton can both tell you, you shouldn't need an apple to hit you on the head to realize a good idea.

In New York City during the seventies and eighties, many minority families and senior citizens couldn't afford their own homes and lived at the mercy of slumlords. Men with reputed links to the Mafia created a corporation that built affordable homes and renovated apartments for them. This wasn't a charitable gesture; the Mob realized no one else was doing shit for poor tenants, and seized an opportunity to land windfall profits.

They spotted a niche and moved fast.

> Organized crime goes where the money is.
> —Howard Abadinsky, organized crime historian

While the Mob was building houses in the Bronx, the Bronx Bombers were attracting hungry hordes of diehard fans.

Wiseguy Matty "The Horse" Ianniello supplied Yankee Stadium's hot dogs. Other mobsters, unable to land a contract as big as The Horse's, were getting wealthy one wiener at a time.

Mobster Philly Dogs operated in Ridgewood, Queens, with hot dog carts planted on all the major intersections. If you watched any of his carts long enough, you'd spot a black Cadillac pull to the curb, a tinted window roll down, and a hand reach out for an envelope. The hand belonged to Philly Dogs.

"I make more money with these carts than my loan shark book," Philly told me. "Everyone loves hot dogs."

At a time when street vending licenses were hard to get, Philly bribed disabled American vets, who received preferential treatment, to apply for the licenses. He had a butcher on the take stealing hot dogs. And his ketchup packets were labeled "Burger King."

Granted, Philly kept his overhead low, but he could have done it legit and still made a small fortune. Ridgewood was a hardworking blue-collar area and Philly had the savvy to see a racket in a dollar a dog for lunch-on-the-go.

> Flexibility and durability are hallmarks of LCN [La Cosa Nostra]. Given a window of opportunity, they will take full advantage of it.
>
> —Frederick Martens

Most of the Mafia's biggest successes started out with only the knack to spot a racket and move fast. Some have figured out how to literally make money coming and going. I knew a guy who was an arsonist for the Mob. He wanted to go legit and used the little money he'd saved to buy a small bulldozer.

After six months' work, he'd saved enough to purchase a full-size bulldozer. A year after that, he bought an excavator. He broke his ass and acquired a couple of big city contracts, then homed in on a real racket: a sand and gravel yard.

Here, he made money coming and going. "I charge people to haul away earth with my machines, then resell it at my yard."

He also got into the demolition business. Today, people pay him to demolish buildings and haul away the wreckage. Back at his yard, he separates steel from concrete and resells it at market value.

A mobster I'll call Joe Puma is now a real estate millionaire living in South America. Long before Puma made his fortune spotting property bargains, he showed his ability to spot a racket.

MOB RULES

One Christmas Eve, I dropped off a bottle of whiskey at Puma's
house. As I walked in, I passed a guy in a Santa Claus outfit on his
way out. Puma thanked me for the bottle and said, "I can use a drink
after handing that fat fuck five hundred to entertain my kids."

"Is that what he makes?" I asked.

"Yeah, I send him to my nephew's house, too." This got me
curious.

"How many houses does he do?"

"At least a dozen. You gotta book him two months out."

The following Christmas Eve, I went to Puma's house to drop off
a bottle. This time, six fatsos were crowded around his living room,
squeezing into Santa suits.

"I know everyone's trying to outdo their neighbors around here,
but you think your kids will believe there's six Santas?"

"I'm makin' twenty G's in four hours. I'll buy my kids a friggin'
reindeer. They'll get over it."

Puma spotted a demand for Santas at Christmastime and knew
that fat men are a surplus commodity in the United States. Whether
through a seasonal Santa business, hot dogs, or trash collection, the
Mob supplies demand every day and on every level.

You might not think of mobsters as the men who feed America,
but their meatpackers and suppliers ship pork, beef, poultry, and even

kosher meats to major supermarket chains. Their trucking companies crisscross the United States delivering every product you can think of. They control the ports and piers, putting seafood on our plates. Their wine and liquor suppliers make sure we have a white or red to wash down all that good food. Their launderers clean the tablecloths in our favorite restaurants, and their jukeboxes play our favorite songs.

"They were almost like a parallel economy in this country," Michael Chertoff, former head of the Department of Homeland Security, said. "There was virtually no area of heavy industrial activity that the Mob was not involved in to some extent. They controlled construction . . . waste carting and garbage removal . . . they were involved in entertainment . . . the hotel unions . . . they controlled the waterfront on the East Coast. They were involved in Las Vegas casinos."

The Mafia men responsible for this parallel economy aren't worthy of the big screen. Business-minded mobsters aren't wild and reckless enough to hold our attention for a two-hour movie. They prefer the shadows and they dress like Mister Rogers. But they're street-smart and they know how to give people what they want.

It's a different side of mobsters, one we're not used to seeing, and they're quite happy not to be seen. They're sated with money, power, and success; who needs notoriety?

Look around your current business environment for areas of untapped profits—jobs others turn their noses up at, markets people don't bother trying to appeal to; there's opportunity everywhere.

If the Mafia had been in ancient Egypt, they would have supplied the stone for the pyramids, unionized the slave labor, put up a sausage and pepper stand, and turned the Sphinx into a casino. They also would have robbed the gold from the pharaohs' tombs; Napoleon later did that himself.

LESSON 12

Roll Up Your Sleeves but Keep Your Pants On

JULIUS Caesar supervised the building of bridges and siege works, marched at the head of an army, and when it came time to fight he rolled up his sleeves and got down and dirty. But off the battlefield, he couldn't keep his toga on. He may have been the first Italian playboy; he screwed everyone's wife, mother, and sister.

Once, while standing on the senate floor, Caesar read aloud a love letter addressed to him from Cato the Younger's half-sister, who was also Brutus's mother.

When Brutus and his coconspirators finally whacked Caesar, Brutus drove his dagger deep into Caesar's groin. "Take that, you pig bastard!"

Twelve hundred years after Caesar's death, the island of Sicily was occupied by a French army. During the occupation, the French conquerors were having their way with the Sicilian women. The Sicilian men bided their time while planning revenge. When they finally struck, the Sicilians cut off the French soldiers' balls and stuffed them in their mouths, a last meal before dying.

Some things never change for Italians: their love of art, architecture, opera, pasta, and cutting people's balls off when they misbehave.

Seven hundred years after the Sicilians served the French their last supper, a man named Michael Devine came on to the wife of a don. Soon after, Devine was found dead, his genitals mutilated, just like Caesar.

Lucchese underboss Anthony "Gaspipe" Casso admitted to killing Anthony Fava, the architect he hired to redesign his home. Casso claimed that Fava, having accepted cash payments, might inform to police, but denied reports that Fava had made a pass at his wife.

Oddly, though, when Fava's body was found, his genitals had been burned with a blowtorch. You decide.

The Mob forbids whoring around with another man's wife or sister. If caught, you may be left with your sausage, but your meatballs are sure to go.

> Pietro was discovered dead in the boot of a car with dollars stuffed in his mouth and his genitals cut off. These Mafia trademarks suggested that he might have been running around with the wife of another Mafioso, a capital offence.
>
> —Tim Shawcross and Martin Young, *Mafia Wars*

Stay away from the boss's goods, or the goods of any coworker. It's the surest way to make enemies, and you'll ruin your career before it starts. There's plenty of fish in the sea. Go catch your own.

LESSON 13

The Walls Have Ears: Never Bad-Mouth the Boss

CICERO, Illinois, was named after the ancient Roman lawyer and statesman Marcus Tullius Cicero. For decades, the town was home base for the Chicago Outfit crime syndicate.

Cicero is considered one of the great Roman orators, and like anyone who likes to hear the sound of his own voice, Cicero often talked too much. Following Julius Caesar's assassination, Mark Antony, a Roman consul, capitalized on Caesar's death and made a grab for power. Cicero spoke out against Antony. In response, Antony had Cicero whacked, his head cut off and hung up for everyone to see.

By doing this, Antony sent a clear message to anyone else thinking about bad-mouthing the boss.

Nearly two thousand years later, Al Capone controlled Cicero, Illinois. When Capone died, his successor running the Outfit was a shrewd mobster named Anthony Accardo. Unlike Capone, who liked publicity, Accardo avoided it, and appointed acting bosses as front men while he pulled their strings behind the scenes.

One of Accardo's front men was Sam Giancana. Once Giancana was appointed acting boss, he made himself a media attraction. To Accardo's dismay, Giancana gravitated toward the limelight. While Giancana was in power, he refused to answer a grand jury subpoena; he was charged with contempt of court and hauled off to the can for a year. This gave Accardo the opportunity to correct his mistake and replace Giancana with a new acting boss. When Giancana was released from the can, he spoke out against Accardo, making it clear to members of the Outfit that he didn't want to relinquish his position.

Accardo, a patient man, knew that Giancana had to be removed. But how and when?

A short time later, Giancana was cooking a meal in his home

when an assassin crept up from behind and shot him several times. Accardo had ordered the hit man to fire five shots in a circle around Giancana's mouth.

By doing this, Accardo sent a clear message to anyone else thinking about bad-mouthing the boss.

History repeated itself. In the town of Cicero, Illinois, Sam Giancana made the same exact mistake as Marcus Tullius Cicero, and bought it in similar fashion.

> Meyer Lansky outlived just about every one of his cronies from the New York Mob, and he did it the old-fashioned way—he kept his mouth shut.
> —*Godfathers Collection: The True History of the Mafia*

Around the same time Giancana got whacked, Mob boss Angelo Bruno was in charge of Philadelphia, where mobster Nicodemo "Little Nicky" Scarfo was coming up in the ranks.

As a young mobster, Scarfo did time with Don Bruno.

Prison has a code of conduct. Items like a book light, sweat suit, or sneakers are considered valuable to a con, but easy to obtain in the free world. Thus, when a convict is released from prison, he leaves his belongings to another inmate, usually someone he was tight with, or a wiseguy from the same crime family.

When Bruno was released from prison, he left Scarfo a handful of paperclips. Just so you know, even in prison, paperclips are worthless.

Although Scarfo knew this was deplorable conduct for a don, Scarfo quietly accepted the "gift" and never uttered a word about it to anyone.

Years later, when Bruno was dead and Scarfo became don of the family, Scarfo repeated the paperclip story to everyone and called Bruno a cheap bastard.

Scarfo wasn't the best don in the world, far from it, but he kept his insults to himself knowing that plenty of mobsters have bad-mouthed the boss and wound up dead.

In the business world, nothing less than your corporate survival is at stake.

Keep this in mind. The walls have ears.

LESSON 14

Did You Wash Your Car or Screw It in the Muffler?: Verbal Skills

A mobster once said to me, "I sodomized my car this afternoon." I was pretty sure he hadn't tapped his car in the ass; he meant he'd Simonized it. I laughed and he realized what he'd said.

Most mobsters have poor linguistic skills. Their vocabulary is limited, and any attempts to use unfamiliar words often end in comedy. But in the professional world, poor use of language can end in tragedy when you don't get that promotion or are relegated to non-communicative tasks.

We think with words, so the broader our vocabulary, the greater our range of thought. A poor vocabulary doesn't mean someone is unintelligent, but a strong vocabulary is indicative of your education, background, and the circles you can move in. The way you speak literally speaks volumes about you and the inner workings of your mind.

> Words can raise the mind to higher things.
>
> —Aristophanes

If you want to impress, develop your linguistic skills. Learning one new word a day, even one word a week, will make a big difference in your speech and, more important, your ability to think.

When I first became a voracious reader, I kept a dictionary at hand and looked up every single word I didn't know. I would write word definitions on a piece of paper, study them, then mull the words over in my mind, using them in different sentences. If conversing with someone who said a word I did not understand, I would shamelessly inquire of its meaning on the spot, or look it up in the dictionary the first chance I got. These practices contributed to expanding my vocabulary and, therefore, my ability to think and express myself.

Although poor speech is acceptable in the Mafia and happens to be the norm, a mobster who speaks well stands out.

> Practice elocution . . . 5–6 A.M.
> —Fictional gangster Jay Gatsby, in F. Scott Fitzgerald's
> *The Great Gatsby*

Don Joe Bonanno once said, "The greatest regret of my life is that I never pushed myself to master the English language. This has proved to be a terrible disadvantage . . . Since I have a limited English vocabulary, I'm forced to simplify my thoughts. Consequently, I come off sounding crude."

At a Commission meeting, Genovese don Anthony "Fat Tony" Salerno commented to Gambino don Paul Castellano, "You talk so beautiful. I wish I could speak like that."

Even the foul-mouthed, cigar-chomping Salerno admired the beauty of speech.

LESSON 15

Count On Yourself and You'll Never Be Counted Out

I'VE met older men who've lived uneventful lives and can boast of having five or six friends they've held on to since childhood. That's great for them, but in the Mob friendships are tested daily; most don't survive.

> When push comes to shove, when a guy's got a gun to his head, that's when you know what he's made of.
>
> —Sam Giancana

On the streets, no man can predict what another man will do when his back is against the wall, but it's a safe bet to put your money on betrayal. That's why a smart mobster, and a smart businessman, makes many friends and builds alliances but never forgets that when push comes to shove he can only count on himself.

An old adage goes, "He who represents himself has a fool for a lawyer." But it's not always true. Plenty of smart mobsters have represented themselves in court because they know that no one, not even a lawyer, can be trusted with their lives.

> Going to trial with a lawyer who considers your whole lifestyle a crime in progress is not a happy prospect.
>
> —Journalist and author Hunter S. Thompson

Carmine "The Snake" Persico was brought to trial in 1985 in a courtroom case dubbed "The Mafia Commission Trial." Persico, with enough cash to fill a fleet of dump trucks, could have afforded any high-profile attorney, but chose to represent himself. It took guts. His life was on the line, but he knew from a lifetime of experience that he could only count on himself in a jam. That's how The Snake was able to master the snake pit of Mafia life.

Jersey mobster Giacomo "Jackie" DiNorscio was put on trial with thirty codefendants for various racketeering charges, including murder. Many of DiNorscio's codefendants hired hot-shot attorneys while DiNorscio represented himself. Nearly everyone at the trial agreed that DiNorscio's Oscar-winning courtroom performance was responsible for the jury acquitting the whole lot.

I wasn't on the streets as long as Persico or DiNorscio, but I also understood that I could only count on myself.

> When I was happy, I thought I knew men, but it was fated that I should know them in misfortune only.
> —Cecil Rhodes

Stuck in the same jam as Persico and DiNorscio, I hired and fired seven lawyers, including the famed civil rights attorney William Kunstler, before I realized that a lawyer will never care as much about my life as I do. I decided to represent myself and soon discovered I could be just as sharp as any attorney; I reversed a federal case my attorney had claimed was impossible to reverse.

Count on yourself and you'll never be counted out.

LESSON 16

How Luciano Became Lucky: Make Your Own Luck

THE kid had a pockmarked face. He worked for five dollars a week. He was arrested for gun possession, armed robbery, assault, gambling, and drugs. Did time in the can. Was shot at. Was knifed, leaving an ugly scar across his cheek. Was beaten senseless while hanging from a rafter. Lived under constant scrutiny of law enforcement. Was exiled. Dead by the age of sixty.

Does this sound like a lucky guy to you? And yet, they called him Lucky. Not sarcastically; they really meant it. How can a guy with a track record like that be called Lucky?

His name was Charles "Lucky" Luciano. And he made his own luck.

As a young boy, Luciano ran errands for anyone who needed an errand boy. He'd run tirelessly back and forth to the grocery store, carrying people's bags to their homes for small change. A Sicilian immigrant who came to America as a kid, Luciano would sit in a theater all day watching silent movies with subtitles to teach himself English.

As a teen, Luciano went to work delivering ladies' hats to department stores. He worked so hard and such long hours that the Jewish owner of the company took him home on Friday nights after work so Luciano could celebrate the Sabbath and at last enjoy a little rest.

While still a teen, and still working hard as a delivery boy, Luciano became a skilled organizer; he put together his own gang and forged alliances with other gangs. He'd later use this skill to work long enduring hours organizing labor unions, and putting together the strongest Mafia family in the world.

> Tony [Spilotro] was a totally focused human being. He had all kinds of financial deals going on at the same time. He had different groups, hundreds of people, a million schemes, all of them in various stages of development. [He] put in a sixteen- to eighteen-hour day trying to put the deals together.
>
> —Nicholas Pileggi, *Casino*

With a penchant for hard work, Luciano has earned the title of the American Mafia's Founding Father. Let's compare Luciano's achievements to one of America's founding fathers, George Washington.

Washington broke America away from British control. Luciano broke the American Mafia away from Sicilian control.

After the Revolutionary War, Washington insisted that Americans remain united, so as not to have another bickering Europe. After Luciano's revolutionary war, he insisted the Mafia remain united and created the Commission to settle disputes and keep all the families working together in harmony.

Washington was offered a crown but refused, knowing the crown would lead to problems. Luciano was offered the title *capo di tutti capi*, boss of bosses, but refused, knowing the title would lead to problems.

Washington's accomplishments inspired the French with their own revolutionary ideas. Luciano's accomplishments inspired the Sicilian Mafia with their own idea of a commission; they called it the Cupola.

All this makes me wonder if Luciano studied Washington's life and tried to emulate it.

George Washington started out just as poor as Luciano. When he was eleven years old, his father died and Washington became the man of the house. By age seventeen, Washington began work as a surveyor, courageously venturing into the wild to define tracts of unsettled land. He learned to live off that land, swam horses across snowy rivers, and forged alliances with wild Indian tribes. By twenty-two, Washington commanded a group of ragtag soldiers and was shooting it out with the French military over land claims.

Like Luciano, Washington would later use his organizational skills and penchant for hard work to piece together an army that defeated the strongest military in the world.

As Washington sat comfortably as the president of a new nation and the greatest revolutionary hero of his time, he may have appeared lucky.

Here's some insight into Washington's "lucky" life at a glance: he rowed his way across the icy Delaware, froze his ass off at Valley Forge, had horses shot out from under him, his coat riddled with bullets, survived a plot to kill him, suffered from illness, fatigue, depression, and anxiety, put down a revolt by his own men, died childless, and had false teeth. Sound lucky to you?

The founding father of America and the founding father of the American Mafia would both tell you that you make your own luck. A study of their lives proves that any luck they got was a product of hard work.

Work hard. Think big. And never lose sight of your goals.

LESSON 17

The Bank of Favors Pays the Highest Interest

DURING World War II, Italian newspaper editor Carlo Tresca railed against fascism and Benito Mussolini. Tresca was living in the United States at the time, where, as a personal favor to Mussolini, Don Vito Genovese ordered a hit on Tresca. The newspaperman was shot down on a Manhattan street. This pleased Il Duce and indebted him to Genovese.

This was a big favor for a big person. Genovese, however, did favors for small people, too.

Yolanda and Sal were like any other newlywed immigrants who arrived in America. They scraped to get by and were happy to live in a tenement on the Lower East Side where they shared a bathroom with half the building.

When Yolanda needed surgery but couldn't afford it, Vito Genovese, the neighborhood don, took care of Yolanda's medical bills.

Like many immigrants at that time, Yolanda and Sal gave birth to a stable of children. One child in particular repaid the favor to Genovese.

> [Lucky] Luciano had few interests in the harbor. [But] Irish hoodlums who operated on the waterfront owed him favors.
>
> —Selwyn Raab, *Five Families*

The child's nickname was Cinzano. As a young man, Cinzano became Genovese's loyal soldier and bodyguard. He'd later become known as "Chin" or Vincent "The Chin" Gigante. When Genovese wanted to eliminate rival Mob boss Frank Costello, he dispatched Gigante. Although Gigante shot Costello in the head, the wound wasn't fatal. Gigante was arrested, kept his mouth shut, and beat the case. He continued to do favors for Genovese and years later, after Genovese died, he assumed control of the Genovese family.

The favor Genovese did for two Italian immigrants paid off in spades. Through Gigante's efficient leadership, the Genovese clan was run like a *Fortune* 500 company.

> The Genovese family is still the most powerful family in the United States and I refer to them as the Ivy League of the underworld.
>
> —Joe Coffey, Organized Crime Task Force

In the straight world, favors don't entail killing newspaper editors or shooting rival Mob bosses.

When I came home from prison, I was legally prohibited from associating with any members of the Gambino family, all of whom formed my old network. In effect, I'd built up a large bank of favors but was denied access to the account.

Fortunately, I was friends with a legitimate businessman on Long Island who has created a massive web of favors in which he is the center.

Like a switchboard operator, John "Johnny Parkway" Brunetti connects you with someone whose help you need. Once Johnny has done a favor for you, you'll more than likely oblige if he asks you to do a favor for someone else, and that's how his circle of favors grows.

> Bonasera: How much shall I pay you?
> Don Corleone: Some day, and that day may never come, I will call upon you to do me a service in return.
>
> —Mario Puzo, *The Godfather*

Johnny Parkway offered me a loan from his bank of favors, putting me in contact with anyone he thought might help me pursue a career as a writer.

Johnny Parkway helps a lot of people. In doing so, he's become successful. He's got good business sense but his circle of favors is what sets him apart from the herd of corporate elites who won't move their asses unless there's an immediate profit involved.

> Favors are like money in the bank with Italians. We collect favors, trade favors, count them like assets, hold them and collect on them.
>
> —Fictional Mafia don Frank Bellarosa,
> in Nelson DeMille's *The Gold Coast*

Keep a stash in the Bank of Favors; you never know when you'll need to make a withdrawal.

LESSON 18

Why "The Chin" Wore Pajamas to Work: When to Play Dumb

WHEN Don Joe Bonanno was subpoenaed to appear before a grand jury, he complained of heart problems and checked himself into a hospital. He was seventy-nine. Despite Bonanno's complaints, the old ticker beat like a Rolex for ninety-seven years, nearly a century. The best engineers at BMW can't make an engine like Bonanno's heart.

During World War II, Joe Colombo faked mental illness to get out of the Coast Guard. He later became don of the family that bears his name.

Anthony "Tumac" Accetturo cried amnesia when he was indicted. After he beat the rap, he claimed he hit his head in the shower and miraculously got his memory back.

The Mafia has more artists than Florence during the Renaissance: bullshit artists. That said, the Mob's Michelangelo was Vincent "The Chin" Gigante, the boss who feigned insanity for thirty years to avoid prosecution.

Aware he was under constant surveillance, Gigante strolled Manhattan in striped pajamas and a bathrobe, talking to parking meters. Gigante even subjected many of his fellow mobsters to his charade.

While Gigante was still a capo, a friend of mine was at a sit-down with him. Gigante, maintaining his silence, had appointed another wiseguy as his mouthpiece. While the discussion carried on, Gigante threw his foot up on the table and began clipping his toenails. As if this wasn't crazy enough, he cut them too short and his toes bled onto the table. My friend left the sit and said, "I know it's an act, but this guy's fucking nuts!"

Gigante's behavior was extreme, as were the consequences he

was trying to avoid, a life sentence in prison. He does, however, illustrate why it's sometimes expedient to conceal the depth of your intelligence.

Whether climbing a Mafia or corporate ladder, you've got plenty of jealous people above you. If you're a threat on their radar, they'll aim their missiles in your direction.

Philly mobster Salvatore Testa was a young, intelligent wiseguy. When a *Wall Street Journal* article described him as a rising star in the Philly Mob, his boss, "Little Nicky" Scarfo, felt threatened and had him whacked.

When working for someone with Scarfo's attitude, all too common in the legitimate world as well, it's wise to conceal the depth of your intelligence and hide your ambitions. It's sometimes the only way to survive.

There was a wacko Roman emperor named Caligula, who whacked everyone.

While Caligula was having degenerate sex, eating like a pig, and killing members of his own court, there was an imbecile standing in the corner watching it all. Sometimes the imbecile mumbled a few words and everyone threw food at him.

A group of conspirators finally got fed up with Caligula's behavior and iced him.

With no emperor to lead the empire, the conspirators needed to appoint someone fast. They looked around the court for a person they could control, and decided to appoint the imbecile everyone had thrown food at. His name was Claudius.

As emperor of Rome, Claudius proved to be nobody's puppet. A sharp emperor, he ruled for thirteen years, built public works, studied law, and oversaw the expansion of the empire, including the conquest of Great Britain.

Some imbecile.

Claudius knew how to survive and prosper in a lion's den. Plenty of mobsters have survived and prospered the same way. Some went on to become boss, like Claudius. And just about every time, nobody saw it coming.

LESSON 19

The School of Hard Knocks: Experience

WHEN I was released from prison, if you were a potential employer looking at my résumé, a few salient facts would have jumped off the page:

- Three violent felonies
- Never worked an honest day
- Never paid taxes
- Never had a credit card
- No higher education
- No trade
- No honest skills
- No driver's license

Shall I continue? To tell the truth, I'd be leery of working for anyone who would hire me in the first place, based on my résumé, anyway. Now here are the credentials that don't show up on my résumé:

- Honorable
- Ambitious
- Resourceful
- Word is gold
- Friends trust him with their lives, and he's proven worthy of that trust
- Refuses to quit
- Never makes the same mistake twice

This last bullet point is key, because the School of Hard Knocks involves countless mistakes—and learning from each.

* * *

FOR decades, Joseph Stalin controlled Russia with an iron fist. In *Young Stalin*, Simon Sebag Montefiore makes references to Stalin's leadership style being similar to that of a Mafia boss:

"Stalin became the effective godfather of a small but useful fundraising operation that really resembled a moderately successful Mafia family, conducting shakedowns, currency counterfeiting, extortion, bank robberies, piracy, and protection-rackets. . . ."

Nikita Khrushchev, who succeeded Stalin, remembered him this way in his memoirs: "I have seen him . . . making mistake after mistake in rapid succession—but never the same mistake twice."

Stalin, a graduate of the School of Hard Knocks, knew that mistakes are part of life, but life is too short and intolerant to allow the same mistakes twice.

ON the drive home from prison, I looked around and noticed much of the world had changed. Family and friends in the car with me were saying, "This changed, that changed. Do you recognize this, do you recognize that? Will you be all right?"

"Have people changed?" I asked.

"No."

"Then I'll be fine."

Human nature is constant. The School of Hard Knocks teaches you this with a high premium on experience, which opens your eyes to a million lessons that can never be learned in a classroom.

> Most of these guys, after all, were just uneducated guys . . . but they were street smart and the thread of the business ran through everything all the time.
>
> —Joe Pistone

Today, I'm confident when promoting myself during a radio or television interview, negotiating a deal, or presenting an idea. I've never been to university but I've got a doctorate from the School of Hard Knocks.

MOB RULES

Here's how I earned it: I began life without a penny in my pocket. My young mother withered away and died in my arms when I was twenty. I survived years in a rat-infested prison rampant with drugs, violence, and sexual abuse. I educated myself inside a dark, damp cell, and re-entered society without a penny in my pocket. After all that, what in the world could shake me?

Here's a little exercise for you; it might be a bit depressing for a few moments but afterward you'll feel invincible. Think of all the tough things you've been through in life: Mom or Dad died, ill child, lost love, messy divorce, survived an auto accident, whatever comes to mind, big or small. When finished, you'll notice you've made it through each and every one of these events, or you're still valiantly fighting. The proof is that you're reading this book. You're no quitter. In fact, you're answering the bell like Bobby Cabert said, and "Ole Blue Eyes" did.

> What you have experienced, no power on Earth can take from you.
>
> —Anonymous

Now tell me, compared with all you've endured, what's a little job interview? How about asking for a raise from the boss? Delivering a product pitch to Walmart? Small potatoes.

You've probably graduated from the School of Hard Knocks and didn't even know it. No diploma, no ceremony, but the notches are in your belt.

By the way, our school has no reunions. We're too tough for that stuff.

LESSON 20

Is This Phone Tapped?: Watch What You
Say Every Day

IN a Manhattan social club, a large banner ran the length of the wall: "THIS CLUB IS BUGGED." On another wall, a large sign with an arrow pointing at a pay phone read, "THIS PHONE IS BUGGED."

One day, I visited the club and noticed that the phone's wire had been clipped.

"What happened?" I asked the wiseguy in charge.

"No matter how many times I warn them," he answered, "they keep bullshittin' on the phone."

Mobsters know not to say anything on the phone that can be used against them in court, yet just about every mobster who gets indicted has phone-tap evidence against him.

> Me, John Gotti, will sever your motherfuckin' head off.
> —John Gotti, Sr., caught on a government wiretap

Guys on the street talk in riddles to try to get around a tapped line. I once overheard a drug dealer say, "I'll take ten kilos of flour and twenty kilos of oregano."

When he hung up the phone, I asked, "What's on your mind? You think the FBI can't figure out you mean cocaine and marijuana?"

"I own a pizzeria," he said. "They can't prove it's drugs."

"Who orders twenty kilos of oregano *from Colombia*?"

I wasn't surprised when he got pinched and went away for forty years.

You shouldn't have to worry about the FBI tapping your phone, but businesspeople record conversations, too. In business, we talk on the phone every day, and we're not always conscious of everything we say. Avoid conversations you don't want played back to you.

In most of the United States, telephone recording laws require that only one party is aware of the recording. Therefore, always speak as if the person on the other line is taping you.

Being a mobster awakened me to the dangers of a telephone. No one is immune. While a mobster's conversation might be played in court, a businessperson's conversation can be played in court, on prime time news, YouTube, pasted all over the Internet, or kept secret and used as blackmail.

Even celebrities are slowly learning to watch their mouths on the phone. In 2008, Kim Basinger taped ex-hubby Alec Baldwin threatening their daughter. In 2010, Mel Gibson, who probably laughed at Baldwin, made the same mistake with his ex-girlfriend.

Of course, you have to watch your text and e-mail messages even more closely.

> Never talk when you can nod. And never nod when you can wink. And never write an e-mail because it's death. You're giving prosecutors all the evidence we need.
>
> —Eliot Spitzer

U.S. Attorney General Alberto Gonzales was forced to resign after a trail of e-mails revealed his knowledge of a politically motivated firing spree of U.S. attorneys.

In the Mob we knew that, even if we didn't have anything bad to say, a few honest words could be misconstrued or twisted. The same goes for the business world. If a benign comment can be taken out of context, imagine what a derogatory remark said in passing can turn into if heard by the wrong ears.

Watch what you say.

LESSON 21

He Should Kill Gus Farace or Kill Himself: Respecting the Chain of Command

IN 1989, Drug Enforcement Agency (DEA) agent Everett Hatcher was working undercover when Mafia associate Gus Farace blew Hatcher's brains out on a Staten Island overpass. Farace took it on the lam and was instantly catapulted from low-level thug to America's Most Wanted.

The feds put the squeeze on the Mob, and the Mob responded to their pressure by marking Farace for death.

Not surprisingly, the Mob located Farace before the feds found him.

Lucchese mobster John Petrucelli, close friends with Farace, had been hiding him. Petrucelli was called in by his capo and told to get rid of the guy.

"I can't do that," he replied.

Word came down from the top. Lucchese boss Vittorio "Little Vic" Amuso said, "[Petrucelli] should kill Farace, or kill himself."

> Their way sure is faster.
> —FBI agent referring to Mafia-style justice.

This is a Mafia boss giving a final decree, not Mr. Whipple telling you, "Don't squeeze the Charmin."

Still, Petrucelli refused—and was killed.

Orders must be followed on every level. When a command is ignored, a soldier or employee must be dealt with. The Mafia is an underworld government; our national government operates by the same strict protocols.

On a Friday afternoon, chauffeured black Cadillacs began lining up in the driveway of a white mansion. Men in dark suits, accompanied by bodyguards, got out of the Caddies and walked into the mansion. They had been summoned by their boss to a secret meeting. Something had to be done about a guy who wasn't following orders.

After some discussion, the men decided that a compromise was out of the question; they needed to "remove the guy."

> I felt terrible that a man with such balls had to be hit. But this was Cosa Nostra. The boss of my family had ordered it. The entire Commission ordered it. There was nothing else I could do.
>
> —Sammy "The Bull" Gravano

The next day, their final decision made headlines: "Truman Fires MacArthur."

General Douglas MacArthur had a supersized ego. His victorious island-hopping campaign against the Japanese during World War II had inflated his head even more. During the Korean War that followed, MacArthur, confident in his own military genius, began ignoring his commander-in-chief, President Harry Truman. MacArthur, a military man, disregarded political considerations that Truman had to weigh daily. Truman, a political product of the Mafia-connected Pendergast Machine, knew how to deal with him.

> Truman owes everything he's got to us. Pendergast made him a judge and then, with the Italian muscle behind him, got him to the Senate.
>
> —Sam Giancana

After consulting with his advisers, Truman removed MacArthur in a scene straight out of a Mob movie, black Caddies and all. Only difference was that the white mansion in question was the White House. In the end, the consequences for disobeying orders were the same—career death.

Whether you look at Don Vic Amuso eliminating Petrucelli or President Harry Truman removing MacArthur, history is filled with object lessons in the importance of following the chain of command. Respect this at the bottom. Enforce it at the top. The alternative is anarchy.

LESSON 22

Go Get Your Own Coffee!: Respecting the Chain of Command Without Being a Sucker

AS you've just read, you must respect the chain of command; orders are orders. But there's a difference between getting serious orders issued for the good of an organization, and being handed a grocery list. True, you must follow orders, but you can't waste half your day at Starbucks ordering Frappuccinos for the boss.

On the streets, I was a good earner and a legitimate tough guy, so I had the respect of other street toughs. Still, I couldn't stop high-ranking wiseguys from trying to play me. I'd draw a line, but telling a wiseguy to "go fuck yourself" isn't good for your health. I avoided confrontations by finding a sensible way to get the same message across, usually by coming up with funny ways to deal with smart-asses.

Here's one situation where I made my point, gained a capo's respect, and got a laugh along the way:

Earlier, we met Gambino capo Robert "Bobby Cabert" Bisaccia, the guy who used to tell me to "answer the bell" while we were in prison together. Bobby and I weren't always so close; our friendship had a rocky start.

Bobby was issued a worn prison uniform that was so wrinkled, it looked like it had been crumpled into a ball before being flattened by a steam roller. Since I was in Bobby's crime family, beneath him in rank, and half his age, he thought he could give me the menial task of ironing his uniform. The problem was that Bobby didn't really know me. I always respected my elders and understood the chain of command, but I was nobody's coolie.

Maybe you didn't hear about it; you've been away a long
time. They didn't go up there and tell you. I don't shine
shoes anymore.

—Tommy DeVito, *Goodfellas*

When Bobby tried to hand me his uniform, I laughed and told
him that I didn't iron my own uniform, but paid another con to do it
for me. I added that I'd happily connect him with my guy.

Bobby ignored my offer and again asked me to iron his uniform.
I smiled, but ground my teeth.

Okay, I said to myself. I'll fix his ass.

I took Bobby's uniform, walked it over to my ironing guy, and
said, "Make this look worse than it does, if possible."

When I returned the uniform to Bobby, I said with a wink, "This
was the best I could do. Hope you like it."

Bobby looked irritated for a moment, then laughed as he realized his mistake. I was a street tough like him, a stand-up guy like
him, and was facing the rest of my life behind bars, like him. If I'd
wanted to iron pants, I'd have gotten a job at a Laundromat. I certainly wouldn't have been sitting in a prison cell.

Once Bobby knew where I stood, we hit it off. I didn't mind making him a cup of coffee, if I was also having one. And Bobby didn't mind
sharing a cup with me, something he'd never do with a coffee boy.

To be sure Bobby harbored no hard feelings, I used my connections at the prison laundry to get Bobby a brand new uniform,
straight out of the box.

In the end, Bobby got what he wanted, a pressed uniform. And I
got what I wanted, the same respect I was willing to give.

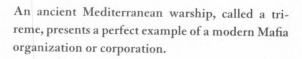

An ancient Mediterranean warship, called a trireme, presents a perfect example of a modern Mafia
organization or corporation.

A trireme had 170 oarsmen on three levels: top, middle, and bottom row. Together these men powered the ship forward.

The ship's captain was known as the trierarch, or CEO.

The ship's overall success, like that of any good company, depended on speed and maneuverability.

The comic playwright Aristophanes tells us, in describing the levels of a trireme, that one row farts in the other's face—not unlike a company.

On the way up, you can put up with a few farts, but never let anyone shit on you.

LESSON 23

Kill or Be Killed: When to Defy Orders

PHILLY don "Little Nicky" Scarfo wanted to whack mobster Salvatore Testa. Scarfo had one of his capos give the contract to Testa's best friend, Joe Pungitore. Pungitore was unhappy with the job, but business was business; he had to do it or he'd be killed himself. He agreed to lure Testa to his death, but refused to pull the trigger.

When Scarfo was told of Pungitore's response, he laughed and said, "What the fuck's the difference?" Scarfo understood that participation in a murder was the same as personally killing someone.

Big corporations don't put contracts out on their employees, but they can perpetrate evil just as effectively as the Mob.

> Don't start talking to me about legitimate business. What about chemical companies dumping all that shit into the rivers and they get all these deformed babies popping up all over the place?
>
> —Tony Soprano, *The Sopranos*

Unlike a member of the Mafia, who must follow orders or be killed, as an employee of a company, you can say no to an unethical demand or assignment. You don't have to deny treatment to an ill person who has no health insurance. You don't have to pick up the phone and harass an old woman drowning in credit card debt. *You* can say no. "No" is such a powerful word that Gandhi, a small man dressed in rags, brought the mighty British Empire to its knees by saying it.

If you're aware of shady business practices and either look the other way or say to yourself, "I'm just following orders," tell me, "What the fuck's the difference?" You're as guilty as the people you work for.

MOB RULES

We have witnessed a level of obedience to orders that is disturbing. With numbing regularity good people were seen to knuckle under to the demands of authority and perform actions that were callous and severe. Men who are in everyday life responsible and decent were seduced by the trappings of authority.
—Stanley Milgram, *Obedience to Authority*

The ancient playwright Sophocles wrote about two brothers, Eteocles and Polyneices, who fought over a kingdom. After the two knocked each other off, some tough guy named Creon snatched the vacant throne.

In a show of partiality to Eteocles, Don Creon declared that he was to be honored with all the funeral rites of a hero, while Polyneices was to be disgraced, left unburied on the battlefield to be eaten by vultures.

Polyneices had a sister, Antigone, who had bigger balls than all the men in the kingdom. In defiance of Creon's edict, she marched onto the battlefield and buried her brother.

Furious, Creon had Antigone hauled before him. She valiantly argued that she'd done the right thing by burying her brother and that, if Creon didn't like it, he could go fuck himself. Enraged, Creon ordered Antigone to be buried alive in a cave.

Antigone botched Creon's slow death decree by taking her own life quickly, a final "fuck you" to the disrespectful don.

In the workplace, there's no Creon to bury you alive, or Scarfo to whack you. Stand up for what's right.

Be an Antigone, not a Pungitore.

LESSON 24

Plato—Didn't He Own a Swingers' Club?: Be Informed

ONE day, an older mobster asked me, "You know who Plato was?"

"Yeah," I said. "He owned a sex joint in New York."

Plato's Retreat was a New York City swingers' club that had operated before my time. I'd heard of the place, figured the old man had a piece, and was about to tell me a story. At the time, I had no idea Plato was also an ancient Greek philosopher. This was okay; after all, I wasn't a philosophy major, but a Mafia minor. On the street, however, it was essential for me to know the history of any person or company I intended to partner with, or shake down.

I once accompanied a wiseguy to a meeting where he was trying to dig his hooks into a businessman. The wiseguy repeatedly knocked the businessman's ex-partner, who both agreed was a lazy son of a bitch and didn't hold up his end of the business.

There's a million harmless ways to express the fact that someone is lazy. This wiseguy happened to choose the only word that could have pinched the guy's nerve. Over and over, he referred to the ex-partner as a cripple. In Mob talk, a "cripple" means a helpless person, someone incapable of earning independently. What the wiseguy didn't know was that the businessman had a son who had been paralyzed in a childhood accident.

If, before the meeting, the wiseguy had inquired about the guy's background, he would quickly have learned to stay away from this distasteful term. (Granted, he should have avoided it anyway.)

Although the businessman never said so, he was obviously disturbed by the reference, and the deal was blown. He found another wiseguy to partner with.

Today, it takes a minute to look someone up on the Internet. If you have a mutual friend or acquaintance, inquire; you might learn some personal tidbits, likes or dislikes, hobbies, anything that might help jump-start a relationship—or might torpedo it before it even begins.

Don't be lazy. Do your homework. Be informed.

LESSON 25

I Want My Fucking Money: Paying Promptly

ONE of the first things I learned from older mobsters was the importance of paying promptly. Any street guy who jerks people around with money earns a reputation as a deadbeat.

When I went to prison, I was owed hundreds of thousands, but didn't owe anyone a nickel because I always paid my debts promptly.

Even people who eventually pay their debts like to hold on to money as long as possible. My belief is, if you've got to give it up, better sooner than later, since you'll look like a star and stand out above the rest.

> He that is known to pay punctually and exactly to the time he promises, may at any time, and on any occasion, raise all the money his friends can spare.
> —Benjamin Franklin, *The Autobiography of Benjamin Franklin*

A good name gets around. Everyone will want to do business with you if you pay on time.

LESSON 26

Don't Tip Your Hand: When to Keep Quiet

DON Carlo Gambino was soft spoken, one of those old-world Mafia dons who sent someone to their grave with a slow nod. In his later years, Gambino shriveled up into a frail old man, and looked anything but dangerous.

One night, Gambino was dining in a Brooklyn restaurant when a wiseguy named Carmine "Mimi" Scialo began to insult him. Scialo was a feared hit man and figured his violent reputation would frighten Gambino. Gambino took the harassment in silence. The old don would never tip his hand and betray his thoughts.

> The marks of a true Mafioso are that he speaks little, makes each word count, and maintains a grave and dignified presence at all times, even under extreme provocation.
>
> —Paul Lunde, *Organized Crime*

Not long after this incident, Scialo's body was found encased in the cement floor of a Brooklyn basement. Everyone in the underworld knew that Scialo died for insulting Gambino.

Seven years later and an ocean away, the Sicilian Mafia was at war.

A hit man, Pino Greco, gunned down Mafia boss Salvatore Inzerillo. Inzerillo died over a power struggle; little more can be said about the cause of his death. However, the death of Inzerillo's seventeen-year-old son, Giuseppe, was a very different story. Young Giuseppe died because he tipped his hand.

At his father's funeral, Giuseppe openly vowed to avenge his father's murder. Giuseppe's threats were not taken lightly. Not long after the funeral, Giuseppe was kidnapped and tortured by his father's killer. Before putting the teenager out of his misery, Greco sawed off Giuseppe's arm and taunted him with it, telling the boy he could no longer use that arm to avenge his father's death.

> [A]n ex-con named Frank Benjamin was heard bragging about how he was going to take out the whole Winter Hill crew. . . . A gunman loyal to Winter Hill shot Benjamin in the head.
>
> —T. J. English, *Paddy Whacked: The Untold Story of the Irish American Gangster*

About seven years after the Inzerillo murders, back on this side of the Atlantic, Mob informant Nicky "The Crow" Caramandi was in the process of testifying in eleven federal trials that ultimately dismantled the Philly Mob.

The feds were hiding The Crow at a posh condo. Two women, mother and sister of two brothers he was testifying against, spotted The Crow sunbathing by the pool. The Crow, however, did not spot them—until the two women started yelling and cursing at him:

"You dirty rat bastard!"

"No good stoolie!"

The Crow took to the air and flew away, never to be seen again. Had the women not tipped their hand, The Crow, or canary, or whatever fucking bird he was, would've taken his final bird bath, floating facedown in that condo pool.

No matter how tempting, don't tip your hand.

LESSON 27

Capone, Harvard, and Yale: The Key to Growth

AL Capone ordered the deaths of hundreds of men and personally killed a few himself. Yet he allowed the hood who'd made chop suey out of his face to live.

When Capone was a teen, he hung out at a New York nightspot called the Harvard Inn, owned by mobster Frankie Yale. One night, a street guy named Frank "Galluch" Gallucio was at the Inn, seated at a table with his girlfriend and his younger sister, Lena. Capone spotted pretty Lena and tried to pick her up. Lena wasn't interested in the chubby, balding, pimple-faced thug, and snubbed him. Capone, not one to give up, kept trying.

After a while, Galluch kindly informed Capone that Lena was his younger sister and asked him to move on. Capone, young and in need of manners, ignored Galluch and told Lena she had a nice ass. Unfortunately for Capone, Galluch handled a knife like a Benihana chef.

Capone was rushed to Coney Island Hospital, and "Scarface" was born.

Surprisingly, Capone didn't seek revenge. He might have been a wiseass, but he knew when he was wrong. The act of admitting he was wrong, even in his teens, showed early wisdom, the kind of wisdom needed to run Chicago's underworld and overworld, including a crooked police force and a political machine. Capone had what it took.

Years later, Al "Scarface" Capone rose to the top of the Mafia's food chain. As don, he had power over life and death and could have ordered "fried eggs and Galluch" for breakfast. Capone not only spared Galluch's life, he hired him as a personal bodyguard whenever he visited New York. As further testament to Capone's character, Galluch trusted him enough to accept the job.

Galluch died of a heart attack in 1960, thirteen years after Capone expired.

It's tough to admit you've made a mistake, but denial is for dummies. Don't worry about your ego, you'll get over it. If Capone did, you can. Admitting you're wrong, even to yourself, is the single most important step toward personal growth.

LESSON 28

The Bug and the Jaguar: Patience

LET'S turn to law enforcement's war on the Mafia for a lesson in patience.

On television and film, cops break down doors and screech around corners in high-speed car chases while firing guns at the bad guys. That's bullshit. Most cops and agents never fire a gun except at the range. Investigative work is tedious and takes a ton of patience, especially work involving a crime family.

A cop or agent investigating a mobster combs through stacks of files and phone records, records license plate numbers, and takes pictures, labeling the photos on a corkboard back at headquarters. I'm getting bored just thinking about the shit they have to do.

> These investigations take years to develop, and one of the strong assets for organized crime agents is patience.
> —Bruce Mouw, former head of the FBI's Gambino squad

But patience pays off, which is why there's always a new Mob pinch in the news.

There is a famous Aesop's fable, "The Tortoise and the Hare," which teaches a lesson about patience. I've given the Mob its own version, "The Bug and the Jaguar."

Salvatore Avellino, the Lucchese mobster who collected Long Island's garbage, spent most of his spare time driving around with his don, Anthony "Tony Ducks" Corallo. Agents investigating Ducks and Avellino decided to plant a bug inside Avellino's Jaguar. The car proved difficult to bug since either Avellino was in the car, or it was locked away in his garage.

The agents sat and waited.

One evening, Avellino went to a banquet at the Huntington Town House on Long Island. He gave the valet a generous tip to keep an eye on his car. Luckily for law enforcement, the valet didn't earn the tip. While the valet chatted on the phone with his girlfriend, listened to the radio, and picked his nose, the agents planted a bug in the Jaguar. The next conversation Avellino had with Corallo was recorded by the FBI. The two wiseguys implicated themselves and others. Patience prevailed; just as the tortoise beat the hare, the bug beat the jaguar.

Agents sometimes surveil a house or hangout for weeks, even months, awaiting that small window of opportunity to plant a bug. Patience on the part of law enforcement is responsible for countless Mafia busts.

I hate to admit it, but when it comes to patience, the law's got one up on the wiseguys.

In all of life, the greatest rewards involve patience.

How poor are they that have not patience!

—Iago, *Othello*

LESSON 29

Stick Your Handouts Up Your . . . :
Cultivate Aggressiveness

FROM youth, I stole, but I never begged. When I realized stealing was wrong, I stopped, but I still never begged.

I was always full of ambition, but horribly misguided. I only needed to harness my wild ambition and direct it toward legal pursuits. Once I did this, I became a new person, but I kept the attitude that I would take what I want—lawfully.

Someone who looks for handouts will develop an "I got it coming" attitude and inevitably become helpless. Believe me, you got nothing coming. I understood this hard truth on the streets, the understanding was reinforced in prison, and it was kicked up my ass when I returned to society, eager to make my way in the straight world.

The Mafia controls labor unions, construction projects, garbage carting, Manhattan's Garment District; they've got their hands in just about every major moneymaking business. Still, as an up-and-comer, I had to pick up a gun and hijack a truck off the street. Just about every Mob boss, including John Gotti, started out this same way, as a hijacker. That's because there are no handouts in the Mob. You've got to make your own way by taking what you want.

> "That's what most people have missed," says a former Chicago chief of detectives. "When you look at Capone or any Italian gangsters back then, the key is the aggressiveness of all the Italians. They would do anything to get ahead."
>
> —Robert J. Schoenberg, *Mr. Capone*

The criminal means by which mobsters acquire wealth is wrong, but their aggressive spirit is right.

Shortly after John Gotti was convicted at trial and given a life sentence, I also became the target of a major racketeering investigation. Certain I would be taken down, I desperately needed a trial defense.

I asked my friend Fat George, the caretaker of John Gotti's Queens hangout, to write a rap song about how Gotti was railroaded by the feds. Next, I contacted a famous rap star and made him an offer he couldn't refuse: create music and teach me how to rap. If I could launch the song before I was indicted, I'd have a defense: I defended John Gotti, and as a result, the feds were now after me.

When the song was completed, I approached Mafia-connected music distributors, all of whom shied away from my endeavor, frightened of the unwanted attention they'd attract. Now what? I knew nothing about the music business. Scrap the project? Lie down and die? Hell no! I picked up the Yellow Pages and began banging on the doors of every music distributor in New York until I found a company that agreed to distribute my song.

> This system of ours gives to each and every one of us a great opportunity if we only seize it with our hands and make the most of it.
>
> —Al Capone

The judge presiding over my case denied me the song as a trial defense, but it was distributed worldwide. And although it didn't help me out of my legal problems, it taught me that if I applied my "take what I want" attitude in a legit way, I could be successful. I used this lesson years later when trying to find my first book publisher.

Every day, go out there and take what you want, just do it the right way.

LESSON 30

Be the Master of Your Own Fate,
Not a Master of Disguises

GAMBINO underboss Aniello Dellacroce was nicknamed "O'Neil," a shortened moniker for Father Timothy O'Neil, a clerical name Dellacroce picked up after he dressed as a priest to carry out a murder contract.

Sicilian boss Bernardo Provenzano showed up at a covert Mob meeting wearing a bishop's robe with miter and sash.

The hit men who shot Irish gangster Punchy McLaughlin in the parking lot of Boston's Beth Israel Hospital were dressed as rabbis.

And a Lucchese hit man masqueraded as a doctor when he tried to finish off Mob stoolie "Fat Pete" Chiodo as Chiodo lay in a hospital bed.

A number of mobsters have changed their identity and become someone else to get a job done, then gone back to their old selves.

Ponder this. If it's that simple to change one's identity for a day, why can't people just as easily change who they are forever?

They can.

The human brain has the amazing ability to change itself. Nearly every cell in our body is replaced with new cells over a period of seven years. More astonishing, it takes a seventh of a second to change one's mind.

At any time in your life, you can make the decision to change and become a new person.

Dellacroce could have become a real priest, and the Lucchese hit man a real doctor, if they had wanted to. Who do you want to be? The same God who created Crick and Watson, Newton and Einstein, Bill Gates and Steve Jobs, also created you.

Can everyone be an Einstein? Science is getting ever closer to solving the complex puzzle that is the human brain. And it's beginning to look as if there's genius in all of us.

—*The Sunday Times* (London)

All the great men and women who've made a mark on this earth were made of the same exact stuff as you. No magic you don't possess, no hocus-pocus; they simply discovered their purpose and busted their asses.

When I decided to become someone new, I ditched my Mafia aspirations and discovered a love for reading and writing. It took many years to develop into a writer, but I wouldn't quit.

Every saint has a past, and every sinner has a future.

—Oscar Wilde

After publishing my first book, *Unlocked*, I was invited to speak and sign books at a book fair in San Francisco. A limousine picked me up from the airport and drove me to my hotel. There were no parking spaces in front of the hotel so I told my driver to double park and pop the trunk.

After removing my suitcase from the trunk, I found myself pinned between the limousine's rear bumper and the front bumper of a truck. The truck driver had pulled up dangerously close to me, not giving me much room to move. Having just hopped out of a limo, he probably thought I was some rich jerk-off and was fucking with me. I laughed it off.

The fact that it was an armored truck also amused me—a bit of a coincidence given my past.

When I shimmied my way out from between the bumpers, I noticed the company name on the side of the armored truck. Before this trip, I had traveled to San Francisco one other time in my life, to stick up an armored truck belonging to this same fleet.

I smiled. After a slew of bad decisions, I had made the right choices in life. It took time and plenty of ups and downs, but I answered the bell, admitted I was wrong, decided to change who I wanted to be, and discovered my purpose.

I'm no neuroscientist, but I felt as though my brain responded to my decision to change and began creating new cells, or rearranging neurons from the configuration of a mobster to that of a writer. I'm no mystic either but I assure you, following my decision, the universe followed suit and all the right doors opened for me.

I accepted the armored truck coincidence as a nod of approval from those mysterious forces we all know exist.

As I walked into the hotel lobby, I glanced back at the truck and said, "Thanks." To myself? To God? To people who helped me? To whom, I'm not sure.

Life is a bunch of decisions. If your first bunch sucks and lands you in the shithouse, start making new decisions until you've gathered up a fresh bunch that brings you to a brighter place. All the mistakes you've made along the way weren't mistakes at all, but experiences. Lessons. As this books proves, you can use every last experience you've lived through, good and bad, to be great at what you finally find you're meant to do.

> I put men to death . . . lost at cards . . . rioted with loose women, and deceived men. Lying, robbery, adultery of all kinds, drunkenness, violence, and murder, all committed by me, not one crime omitted . . . such was my life.
> —You would suspect this to be the confession of a Mafia informant, not an excerpt from *My Confession*, autobiography of Leo Tolstoy, acclaimed author of *War and Peace*.

We are all made of the same stuff.

PART II

LESSONS FOR A CAPO
(MIDDLE MANAGEMENT)

Cosa Nostra and affiliates are as big as U.S. Steel, the American Telephone and Telegraph Co., General Motors, Standard Oil of New Jersey, General Electric, Ford Motor Co., IBM, Chrysler and RCA put together.

—*Time* magazine

LESSON 31

Bacon, Lettuce, and DeMeo: You're Responsible for Your Crew

IN the late seventies and early eighties, Gambino wiseguy Roy DeMeo headed a murderous Brooklyn crew. The scent of blood gave DeMeo a hard-on. In addition to Mob hits, DeMeo killed innocent people, proving he was a demented serial killer masquerading as a gangster. His Mafia superiors, including his capo Nino Gaggi, overlooked his psychopathy because of his knack for disposing of the family's unwanted problems.

In 1977, when DeMeo was just beginning his rampage, he did some stolen car business with a hood named John Quinn. When Quinn got pinched, he decided to flip. DeMeo got wind of Quinn's defection and invited him to a meeting at the Brooklyn lounge where DeMeo and his crew chopped up most of their victims.

Quinn arrived at the lounge accompanied by his teenage girlfriend, Cherie Golden.

As Golden waited in Quinn's parked car, Quinn went inside the lounge and was shot in the head. While Quinn's body was being butchered inside, two of DeMeo's crew members approached Golden outside and started to bullshit with her. They were slick talkers, and Golden had no reason to be concerned—until one of them pulled out a gun and shot her in the face. The other man shoved her dead body onto the floorboard under the glove compartment, as casually as one would an empty McDonald's bag. They dumped her and the car, then returned to the lounge to help dismember Quinn's body. It was a typical day's work for DeMeo and his crew.

According to the Mob's rule book, eliminating a snitch like Quinn is mandatory conduct. Blowing away a snitch's nineteen-year-old girlfriend is another story; the Mob does not condone that kind of behavior.

The murder of Cherie Golden made the newspapers. When Gambino boss Paul Castellano learned through the streets that DeMeo was responsible, he summoned DeMeo's capo, Nino Gaggi, demanding an explanation.

Every man is responsible for the actions of his crew, so Gaggi would have to either kill DeMeo or convince Castellano that the murder was justified. Gaggi was earning big with DeMeo, so he decided to plead his case.

Gaggi told Castellano that Golden was a potential informant, privy to Quinn's criminal affairs, and had been disposed of to protect the family. DeMeo's large profits passed through Gaggi's hands into the palm of Castellano, so, blinded by the bacon, Castellano swallowed Gaggi's lame excuse and allowed Gaggi and DeMeo to live.

A good boss holds his capos responsible for their own actions as well as the actions of anyone under their command. Castellano did not assign responsibility to anyone involved in the Golden murder, and for that he would pay dearly.

A short time later, Gaggi and DeMeo became entangled in a federal racketeering indictment that also netted Castellano. At this point, Castellano grew angry with DeMeo, blaming the indictment on DeMeo's recklessness. (Note that Castellano wasn't nearly as concerned with DeMeo's recklessness when Golden was the victim.) On Castellano's orders, DeMeo was murdered, but it was too late: the damage to Castellano could not be undone.

Unlike Castellano, Bonanno family boss Joseph Massino ran a tight ship; every capo was truly responsible for the actions of his crew. Period.

Around the time DeMeo, Gaggi, and Castellano were passing winks over the murder of a teenage girl, the Bonanno family was infiltrated by undercover agent Joe Pistone, aka Donnie Brasco.

The movie *Donnie Brasco* didn't win any Academy Awards, but real-life agent Joe Pistone deserved one for his acting. Pistone bullshitted his way into a Bonanno crew headed by capo Dominick "Sonny Black" Napolitano.

After a long investigation, Pistone's identity was deliberately revealed. The Bonanno mobsters who had mistakenly accepted Pistone into their crew all knew that with Massino at the helm their fate was sealed.

The first to walk the plank was wiseguy Anthony "Tough Tony" Mirra. Mirra had been the first to bring Pistone around and introduce him to everyone. To Mirra's credit, he knew he was a dead man, but he didn't turn stoolie. Mirra was killed by both his families, the Bonanno family who ordered the hit, and his immediate family, his nephew and uncle, who carried it out.

Don Massino wasn't done making his point.

Dominick "Sonny Black" Napolitano was next to go. Napolitano didn't bring Pistone around and was duped like everyone else, but that didn't matter to Massino. Napolitano was responsible for his crew, and anything that went wrong under his command was his fault. Like Mirra, Napolitano knew his fate but didn't flip. He accepted responsibility for his crew, and paid for their error with his life.

Massino sent a clear message to anyone considering the excuse, "It's not my fault." Had Castellano acted in the same manner, he might still be alive today. Castellano's failure to enforce rules was a sign of weakness his future murderers took careful note of.

Castellano should have had DeMeo's head delivered to the doorstep of Cherie Golden's family. Instead, he turned a cheek, reached out his hand, and took another envelope. Bum.

If you work for a good company, if you're under a sharp boss, know that everything is your responsibility.

During World War II, Prime Minister Winston Churchill gave speeches referring to Hitler and his Nazi thugs as "gangsters."

Hitler was little more than a Mob boss, using violence and intimidation to control the German nation. He bullied most of Europe into submission and refused to heed the battlefield advice of his competent field marshals. When defeat was imminent, Hitler acted like a Mob boss turned rat; he blamed everything on everyone else.

After Germany was reduced to a pile of rubble, Hitler had the balls to say the German people were unworthy of his leadership and deserved what they got. Talk about denial.

Before blowing his twisted brains out, Hitler left a suicide note that claimed he never wanted war, and none of it was his fault. Whose fault was it, Stewie Griffin from *Family Guy?*

Great men accept responsibility for their own mistakes, as well as the blunders that occur under their command.

General Dwight D. Eisenhower, Supreme Allied Commander, was charged with the task of taking down the Nazi Mob boss.

Few people know that Eisenhower prepared a speech in which he accepted full responsibility for the Normandy landings in the event the operation failed. Any general under Ike's command could have fucked up the whole thing, but Ike knew, as Supreme Allied Commander, that he was responsible for everyone under him.

The operation was a success, and the Mob boss was eventually deposed, which meant that Ike did not have to recite his speech to the public.

Winners accept responsibility, learn from mistakes, and move forward.

Losers drown in their own denial, sometimes their own blood, like Don Adolf Shitler.

LESSON 32

How to Hit Your Target Without a Gun:
Motivating Your People

WHEN the U.S. Attorney's office prosecutes a racketeering case, they often designate the leader of the crew the "mastermind."

If you think about it, "mastermind" seems like a word more appropriate to describe Stephen Hawking, not some criminal. But in a way the title is apt: it describes the one mind on the indictment able to master the other minds.

When a Mafia crew is convicted in court, the judge usually gives the mastermind a lengthier sentence than his codefendants because the judge knows that the other conspirators would seldom, if ever, have kicked their own asses into gear. The judge recognizes that most people need someone else to come up with an idea, formulate a plan, and motivate them into action. That someone is the mastermind.

In my racketeering indictment, I was labeled the mastermind by federal prosecutors. It was true. I came up with an idea, sold it to my crew (which made me a master salesman), then motivated them to believe the idea could be realized.

I was astonished to find that men in my crew seldom thought past their upcoming plans for the weekend. With no vision of their own, they were in need of direction, loose clay waiting to be molded. This may or may not surprise you, but men in my crew represent the majority of the world's employees. It's up to you to become their mastermind.

> Few men have any next; they live from hand to mouth, without a plan, and are ever at the end of their line, and, after each action, wait for an impulse from abroad.
> —Ralph Waldo Emerson

Whether in the Mob or the real world, people without vision don't believe they have the ability to accomplish big things; in essence, they don't believe in themselves. However, if they believe in you because you've emerged as a leader, then you can instill in them a strong sense of confidence and motivate them by assuring them, *"We* can do this!"

We presents them with an opportunity to latch on to your shirttail and accomplish something with you. If they believe in you, they'll now believe in themselves.

Through strong leadership and proper motivation, you can galvanize a dozen or so people and magnify your own one-cylinder ambition into a twelve-cylinder locomotive, ready to plow through any mountain.

LESSON 33

Let's Meet in the Back for a Sit-down: Mediating Disputes
and the Art of Compromise

THOSE who know the Mafia only through the media will probably
have trouble believing that the Mob goes to great lengths to avoid
violence.

> The "Docile Don," Angelo [Bruno] hated violence and valued negotiation and peace above all.
> —George Fresolone and Robert J. Wagman,
> ***Blood Oath***

The Mob's main instrument for resolving disputes is called a "sit-down." Sometimes, two men of equal rank will sit down together to air out their grievances. If they're unable to reach a compromise, then someone who holds a position of authority in the family, similar to middle management, will preside over the sit. It's understood going into the sit that this mediator's decision is final.

Surprisingly, the criminal characters who preside over sit-downs are fair and judicious in their judgments, which is the reason the sit works and remains revered.

> At first, The Chin disagreed with Casso . . . they talked back and forth. Ultimately, The Chin agreed with Casso's position because what Casso said was just and reasonable.
> —Philip Carlo, ***Gaspipe: Confessions of a Mafia Boss***

All day long, mobsters bump heads on the street. Every beef is brought to the table, from a stolen bottle of whiskey to a billion in stolen bonds. People fight over everything, especially when there's money involved.

Aside from money, the sit can settle a beef over a man's reputation, a question of respect, even squabbles between mobsters' wives and daughters.

I once took part in a sit-down I'll call the "Breakfast Beef." This street guy named Bruno woke up with a hangover and ordered his wife to cook him breakfast. His wife smelled another woman's perfume on his clothes and slapped him across the face with a slab of raw bacon. Bruno, in turn, broke a dozen eggs over her head, then repeated his order to make him breakfast. His wife, shells stuck in her hair, yoke on her face, began to fry the bacon.

While the bacon sizzled, she called her brother, Joey, a street guy in my crew. Joey lived nearby and showed up at her house minutes later. Almost immediately, Joey and Bruno began fist fighting in the kitchen. At some point, Bruno was hit with the hot pan of bacon grease and suffered serious burns.

When Bruno got out of the hospital, he wanted Joey dead and put in a beef. I sent Joey into hiding and defended him at the sit. According to Mob rules, Joey was permitted to defend his sister, but Bruno argued that Joey, by burning his face, had gone too far. I argued that Joey's sister, not Joey, hit Bruno with the grease. After all, I said, Joey's sister was an abused wife who could do as she pleased, unfettered by Mob rules. Bruno now looked like an abusive husband who got what he had coming, and Joey was off the hook.

Within a month, Bruno had divorced Joey's sister. No policemen, no lawyers, no civil suit, no drawn-out divorce proceedings. The outcome of a large problem involving three lives was settled in less than an hour, because it's agreed upon in the Mob that everyone must make a serious attempt at resolving differences.

Imagine a world in which people sit down and discuss their problems, walking away from the table with a resolution that same day. This is the world of the Mafia.

The Mob knows that grudges interfere with growth, and

simmering disputes boil over into serious trouble. Take a lesson, and be quick to arbitrate between coworkers. Make people talk out their differences. Squash a beef before it gets out of hand, and be sure to offer fair and honest advice every time. Learn from the Mob's tireless efforts at diplomacy, the most powerful weapon in their arsenal.

> Whatever happened in the past is over. There is to be no more ill feeling among us. If you lost someone in this past war of ours, you must forgive and forget.
> —Salvatore Maranzano, following the Castellammarese War, as quoted by Joseph Valachi

LESSON 34

When to Take a Bullet for the Boss

MANY mobsters wholeheartedly believe in The Life, the chain of command, death before dishonor, and are willing to sacrifice themselves for the good of the organization.

Other mobsters temper ideology with self-preservation, and will only take a bullet for the boss if it benefits them in the long run.

> Organized crime is a non-ideological enterprise.
> —Howard Abadinsky ·

The latter is the best and only approach in the business world.

Before taking a bullet for the boss, consider that you may not be repaid for your sacrifice. Like anyone else, your boss has a track record. Does he stand by his employees? Support them? Did he achieve his position by stepping on the backs of others?

Knowing how your boss has treated those who have made sacrifices for him in the past should help you decide. There should be a lot of evidence to suggest your sacrifice will be rewarded before you take that bullet. In short, weigh your long-term benefits against your short-term sacrifice.

LESSON 35

Why Hit Men Tell Jokes over a Dead Body:
Bonding with Subordinates

IN 1981, Bonanno soldiers Frank Lino and Stefano "Stevie Beef" Cannone picked up capo "Sonny Black" Napolitano and drove him to a house where Napolitano was to be killed.

As the three men walked up to the porch, mobster Frank Coppa opened the front door and directed them into the cellar. Downstairs, Robert Lino, Sr., and Ronald "Monkey Man" Filocomo were lying in wait.

Napolitano was kicked down the steps, shot, and killed.

Parked in a van outside the house where this was taking place were Joseph Massino, Salvatore Vitale, and George Sciascia, there as backup shooters in case anything went wrong. Several other mobsters picked up Napolitano's body and disposed of it.

A dozen men to kill one man. Why was this simple hit turned into a family affair? Bonding. Everyone dips their hands in the blood.

> In all illegal enterprises, criminal or political, the group, for the sake of its own safety, will require that each individual perform an irrevocable action in order to burn his bridges to respectable society before he is admitted into the community of violence.
>
> —Hannah Arendt, *On Violence*

Mobsters have many ways to bond that don't involve killing. Everyday bonding rituals include poker, bocce, baseball, and vacations. Manhattan's Feast of San Gennaro is like a Mafia company picnic. The Mafia is a "family," and a family that plays together, stays together.

Businesspeople bond by playing together, too. A two-seater golf cart is the perfect vehicle for bonding. Contracts are signed at the office, but deals are hatched on the greens.

My friend Tony Licatesi owns a large law firm. He takes clients to Yankee games. Besides dazzling them with impressive seats, he's got three hours to woo them. Whether the Yanks win or lose, Tony leaves the stadium a winner.

Another friend of mine has weekly card games at his house, just like we did in the Mob. Food, drink, jokes, and laughter, a great way to bond.

Truth is, adults like to play as much as children and adults are bound together more by interests than by friendship.

In a relaxing environment, we drop our guard and realize how much we have in common with one another. Sure, professional behavior is critical in the workplace, but strengthening your bond with your colleagues is conducive to progress. It's just easier to deal with people to whom we can relate. And we discover our common ground through bonding.

> That day, Tony and I weren't gangsters, thieves, shylocks, or enforcers, just friends. We loved our families, we loved the idea of loyalty, we even loved each other. The streets, the whole Mob thing, gave us a sense of honor and camaraderie we both needed.
>
> —*Unlocked*

LESSON 36

Nino Gaggi's Magic Bullet:
The Mob Never Kills a Good Idea

GAMBINO capo Nino Gaggi had a beef with another wiseguy in the family. Because the other wiseguy had previously broken Mafia rules and was already on the outs with the boss, a sit-down was bypassed and Gaggi received direct permission from his don to whack the guy.

Gaggi set up the hit, but it didn't go according to plan. The two were driving on the Belt Parkway in Brooklyn when the wiseguy suddenly realized he was being driven to his execution, and not a meeting as Gaggi had claimed. The wiseguy tried to get Gaggi to stop the car. Instead of canceling the hit, Gaggi pulled the trigger there and then. While motorists drove by, Gaggi got out of the car and walked away, leaving the body in the car, parked on the shoulder.

A young motorist who witnessed the incident took the next exit off the parkway and flagged down a cab, hoping to use the cabbie's radio to call for help. It so happened the cabbie was an armed, off-duty cop moonlighting as a cab driver.

The cop drove around until he spotted a man who fit Gaggi's description, bloody clothes and all. He drew his gun and identified himself as a cop. As should already be clear, Gaggi didn't like anyone interfering with his plans; he squeezed off three shots at the cop, but missed, perhaps because he was accustomed to firing his weapon at point-blank range. The cop returned fire and dropped Gaggi, a bullet lodged in his neck.

After a trip to Coney Island Hospital, Gaggi was charged with murder and sent to Rikers Island. It looked as though Gaggi's fate was sealed.

Though Gaggi's crew was not Mensa material, they came up

with plenty of creative ideas on how to break him out of the Alcatraz-style fortress.

"We'll get some scuba gear and sneak up on Rikers Island, and take the hospital with machine guns" was one idea briefly tossed around. Picture a group of overfed mobsters stuffed into wetsuits with silk socks and flippers, chomping on soggy cigars. I'm not sure if Gaggi's crew saw the same ludicrous image I did, but they still scrapped the idea.

After floating a few other half-baked plans, Gaggi's crew decided to exchange the bullet lodged in Gaggi's neck for another one. Ballistics evidence would then rule out the cop's gun as the one that fired the bullet into Gaggi. Once the cop was dismissed as Gaggi's shooter, Gaggi could claim he was shot in the neck before the cop even fired at him, arguing that whoever wounded him must also have killed the wiseguy in the car. In court, Gaggi would portray himself as a hapless victim who felt lucky just to be alive.

This magic bullet idea may seem ridiculous, but if you study the evidence presented to the committee that investigated the assassination of JFK, I assure you, Gaggi's magic bullet was a lot less magical than Kennedy's.

Gaggi's crew snuck their magic bullet into the prison visiting room, wrapped inside a condom, and passed it to Gaggi. If Gaggi wasn't already feeling like a scumbag, this should have clinched it. There's irony in everything we do.

Back in his cell, Gaggi clawed at the bullet in his neck. The bullet popped out like a zit and Gaggi flushed it down the toilet. He then called a hack, and handed him the magic bullet, claiming it had just fallen out of his neck.

As it turned out, Gaggi didn't have to rely on his "magic bullet" defense at trial. A young female juror was about to marry a guy whose father was one of Gaggi's loan shark customers. A couple of raspy phone calls later, and the fix was in. Gaggi was acquitted of murder.

(Note the power of networking as related earlier; it's all about who you know.)

Until Gaggi's acquittal, he and his crew entertained any idea that might free Gaggi, however stupid. The most successful mobsters work with ideas, not products. Every major scheme or crime the Mafia ever came up with was spawned from these four simple words: "I got an idea." It's the most quoted phrase I ever heard in the Mob and makes everyone suddenly stop and listen.

During the second Colombo War, an aged and ailing capo, Gregory Scarpa, Sr., tried unsuccessfully to arrange a meeting with leaders of the opposition.

Scarpa's plan was to have an underling push him into the meeting room in a wheelchair, a blanket draped across his lap. Beneath that blanket, Scarpa would have concealed two submachine guns he would use to reduce the opposition to pulp.

From all appearances, Scarpa was a sick old man in a wheelchair, but he could suck your blood with the same teeth he kept in a glass at night. (Respect your elders but always remember that the oldest, most decrepit lion in the jungle can still eat you for breakfast.)

Another pea-brain idea during that same Colombo War came from two gangsters who were unable to get the jump on their target. They planned to hijack a helicopter, then order the pilot to pick up a car magnet from a junkyard. Using that magnet suspended from the helicopter, they would lift their target's car while he traveled on the Belt Parkway. I wouldn't have believed this one myself if I hadn't heard the actual conversation, caught on tape and handed over as evidence before their trial. (The tape should have been used to commit them to an insane asylum.)

As crazy as these Colombo War ideas may sound, some ideas proposed during the First and Second World Wars were just as preposterous. The few ideas that did materialize, however, decided the outcomes of both wars.

During World War I, Lt. Col. Ernest Swinton of the British Army proposed that steam tractors be fitted with armored shells to deflect machine gun and artillery fire and driven into enemy lines. Many laughed, but the idea morphed into the modern tank, a decisive weapon in nearly every major war since. During World War II, the development of an atomic weapon was at first considered by many a ridiculous idea. Yet it ultimately brought the war to a close in the Pacific Theater.

Whether the Allies or the Colombos, soldiers and commanders who displayed the rare ability to think outside the box often stumbled upon great ideas that tipped the scales in their favor.

Think. Encourage others to think. And remember that even the simplest idea can change how we do business. Some have changed the world. Who opened more doors than the inventor of the hinge?

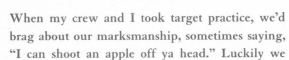

When my crew and I took target practice, we'd brag about our marksmanship, sometimes saying, "I can shoot an apple off ya head." Luckily we never tried this.

Back then, I didn't know where the saying originated. Later on, after becoming an avid reader, I read the story of William Tell, who actually shot an apple off his son's head.

Friedrich Schiller wrote the famous story but got the *idea* to transcribe the legend from another writer named Goethe, who was a big *idea* man.

One day, Goethe was strolling along the street with Beethoven, another big *idea* man. The two idea men crossed paths with the empress and a few dukes. Goethe took off his hat and stepped aside, allowing royalty the right of way. Beethoven walked straight through the crowd, refusing to yield an inch.

Afterward, Beethoven said to Goethe, "There's plenty of them but only two of us. Let them move."

Goethe needed to be reminded by Beethoven that idea men are rare, even rarer than royalty.

LESSON 37

Toss the Dice High:
Dealing with Unreasonable Ultimatums

JULIUS Caesar was becoming a hot-shot general in the field when, back in Rome, senators jealous of his fame and success issued him an ultimatum: "Lay down your command and return to Rome, or suffer the consequences."

Caesar knew it was an unreasonable ultimatum. If he didn't obey, he'd be labeled a traitor and marked for death. If he did return to Rome, the Senate would do away with him anyway. He decided to fight it out.

"Toss the dice high," Plutarch tells us Caesar said before crossing the Rubicon on his way back to Rome. Caesar entered Rome with his army, dissolved the Senate, and overthrew the Republic.

Caesar gambled, and what could have resulted in disaster became his greatest triumph yet. He was later whacked, but that was for something else.

When John Gotti was still a capo, his brother Gene and his close friend Angelo Ruggiero were members of his crew. The authorities recorded tapes of Angelo making drug deals, and the tapes also implicated Gene. Besides the legal ramifications, Gene and Angelo now had a problem with the Gambino family, since drug dealing was forbidden. The tapes were given to Gene and Angelo as evidence in their upcoming trial. Gambino boss Paul Castellano demanded that Gotti get the tapes and hand them over to him so he could review them and pass judgment.

Gotti was faced with an unreasonable ultimatum: deny his boss's request and die for his disobedience, or hand over the tapes, which would lead to the murders of his brother and close friend.

What would you do?

Gotti ripped out a page from Caesar's playbook and "tossed the dice high."

He quickly planned and executed the hit of the century. In one night, Gotti decapitated the Gambino family, killing the boss and underboss in a hail of gunfire.

None of us like to take big gambles with our livelihoods. But, if given an unreasonable ultimatum in work or in life, sometimes your only real alternative is to "toss the dice high" and see where they land.

Knowing we're creatures who grow complacent with our lot, fate may entangle us in a mess, and present us with an unreasonable ultimatum, forcing us to move on in order to lead us in a new direction.

If you're a good person, the loss of your job usually means that a better one awaits. If you're a person with little faith in destiny, this may seem outrageous to you. I assure you, everyone has a destiny. Don't let cowardice interfere with yours.

Like Caesar and Gotti, toss the dice high.

LESSON 38

How to Bury the Hatchet—but Not in Someone's Head

SOME of the greatest partners in organized crime began as enemies.

Salvatore Lucania, later known as "Lucky" Luciano, was only a teen when he started a protection racket in Manhattan. Luciano and his gang threatened and beat up kids unless they paid him a weekly tribute.

One day, a little Jewish boy named Meyer was dragging his way through the snow along downtown Hester Street when he was surrounded by Luciano and his menacing gang. Meyer was threatened with violence if he didn't agree to Luciano's terms. Meyer told Luciano and his gang to go fuck themselves.

This defiance should have resulted in Meyer leaving Hester Street on a stretcher. Instead, Luciano was sharp enough to realize that an alliance with the brazen little Jew might prove advantageous for himself. Luciano offered Meyer his hand. Meyer shook, and the greatest partnership in organized crime was forged. The two young men, Lucky Luciano and Meyer Lansky, went on to dominate the rackets for decades.

Lesser men would've exchanged blows and cursed each other for the rest of their lives.

Louisiana Mob boss Carlos Marcello was pulled over for speeding, and the hot-shot cop waved a gun in his face. At the time, Marcello had tight control over many of Louisiana's politicians and could have had the cop transferred to Alaska. He also could have sued the city of New Orleans for harassment.

But only petty men are concerned with petty satisfactions. Marcello, a large man in a small body, drove over to the police officer's post the next day and gave the cop a gold pistol-shaped cigarette lighter. "Since ya like to wave ya gun so much."

The gung-ho cop was compromised, and Marcello went about his business of empire building. Marcello had a knack for turning enemies into friends.

In business, as in life, it's important to know that even sworn enemies can resolve differences and prosper together.

> [Hymie] Weiss, notably smarter, might see through his own hotheadedness to the business sense of forgiving and forgetting.
>
> —Robert J. Schoenberg, *Mr. Capone*

A true enemy must be defeated. But there are few, if any, true enemies. It's usually a question of stubborn pride and an unwillingness to compromise.

The American Civil War claimed over six hundred thousand lives, dividing the country, states, even immediate families.

After the Union won, the Confederates were granted an "unconditional pardon."

Because of the pardon, archenemies from the North and South were able to collaborate and create a new country that, less than fifty years later, was attractive enough to lure European immigrants en masse.

Two such immigrants who arrived in New York at this time were Salvatore Lucania and Meyer Lansky. A compromise of their own would prove as monumental in the underworld as the national compromise was for our overworld.

Forgive your enemies. It's the smart thing to do.

LESSON 39

Take That Stone from My Shoe: Firing and Hiring

THE title of this chapter is an old Sicilian saying which roughly translates as, "Get rid of that pain in my ass." When a Mafia boss says it, it's curtains for somebody. But the boss doesn't kill everyone who screws up. Sometimes, a mobster is "put on the shelf." When a don shelves someone, it's like a papal excommunication; no one can have anything to do with the guy. He's lost his authority, and can't make a buck.

Gambino mobster Carmine Lombardozzi was a wild man the family was having difficulty controlling. On one occasion, Lombardozzi slugged a cop in the face. On another, he attacked an FBI agent who was snooping around at his father's funeral.

Lombardozzi's anger may have been justified in each case, but the family doesn't allow its members to attack law enforcement officers, which only brings heat. His don put him on the shelf, or "broke him," meaning he was fired.

> A Man of Honour can be expelled for reasons relating to the family he belongs to or the Mafia organization as a whole. It is considered a very grave mistake for a Man of Honour to continue to deal and even talk to a member expelled for not being worthy.
> —Tim Shawcross and Martin Young, *Mafia Wars*

A wiseguy who is shelved can be taken off the shelf if he convinces his don he's worthy of a second shot. And in the end, Lombardozzi wasn't beyond redemption. He lay low for a while to let the family's anger abate, and then approached his don with a sincere apology and a promise to fall in line.

Once reinstated, Lombardozzi worked his ass off for the family, expanding the Gambinos' sphere of influence into the stock market and becoming known as "The King of Wall Street."

The wildest colts make the best horses.

—Plutarch, *Life of Themistocles*

Once taken off the shelf, Lombardozzi proved much more valuable than before, while all his don had wanted was a little more discipline.

Sometimes you've got to shelve or fire someone. Strictly business, right? But consider taking that former employee back if it benefits the business. The second time around, you may end up with twice the worker. The Mob does it, why shouldn't you?

In the eleventh century, King Henry IV of Germany had a few Lombardozzi-style issues with discipline. As a result, he was excommunicated, or shelved, by Pope Gregory VII.

Unhappy with this ostracism, Henry sought an audience with his boss, the pope.

In the dead of winter, Henry crossed the Alps with his queen and young son, carrying them over mountains and gliding them across frozen lakes.

At last, Henry reached the fortress of Canossa, where the pope sat comfortably within its walls, warming his slippered feet before a fire while chewing on a lamb chop.

Wearing nothing but a shirt, Henry stood barefoot in the snow, freezing his ass off for three long days until the pope came to the door.

Moved by Henry's sincere apology, the pope lifted the excommunication (gave Henry his job back or took him off the shelf), ripped a fart, and slammed the door.

If you mess up and know it, it's okay to ask for your job back. Lombardozzi did it and so did a king. Just don't go as far as Henry, you'll end up in the nuthouse; in the Mafia, a trunk.

By the same token, if you're in a position to play pope or don, consider an apology. We all make mistakes.

LESSON 40

The Toughest Guys Have the Thinnest Skin: Never Embarrass Someone in Public

COMING up in the Mob, I was filled with ambition, but not with experience. When I screwed up, I was fortunate to be around old-timers who knew enough to lecture me in private, and never embarrass me in front of other people. I was able to learn my lessons without being shamed in the process.

Even with my Italian machismo, Mafia hubris, and Napoleon complex, I was always open to advice or criticism—as long as it was done with tact. If someone had exposed my mistakes in front of others, I would have been angry and ashamed, and more important I would have dismissed their sound advice, unable to think beyond my emotions.

Mobsters have emotions like everyone else; in fact, some are downright touchy. I've been up close and personal with killers, and they have the thinnest skin of all. They just hide their sensitivity behind a tough-guy persona. That's why a stone-cold killer's reaction to even a minor insult can be deadly. Knowing this, their bosses might correct them in private, but never embarrass them in public.

Employees aren't volatile hit men, but they can still blow their stacks, suffer embarrassment, or harbor an eternal grudge.

If someone screws up, correct them in private.

LESSON 41

The Mafia Isn't Turning Yellow, but Going Green: Keeping Up with the World

I went to prison in 1994 and came home in 2003. While I was away, billions of people began using mobile phones, iPods, and the Internet. At first, I didn't understand the latest technology. After all, I'd been in a cave.

Although I didn't return to The Life, I still bumped into mobsters now and then. I once ran into a wiseguy in Starbucks sitting with a latte and a laptop. I surmised that, like me, he'd also left the Mob. Not so. He asked me if I wanted to place a bet on any sports games. I said no and sipped my coffee as he rattled off some figures into his Bluetooth headset, punched a few keys on his computer, and removed his flash drive.

"You're really up-to-date," I said.

"Offshore gamblin'," he replied. "I got forty people workin' for me in Central America, an' I never been there. This drive"—he held up the flash drive—"has a million dollars in action on it. An' I can hide it anywhere." He tucked it into his sock.

Time and again, I'm astonished by humankind's latest technological advances. What hasn't surprised me is the Mafia keeping up with the times.

In his book *My FBI*, former top fed Louis Freeh tells us, "Japanese crime syndicates have used Russian hackers to blast their way into police databases so they can monitor efforts to rein them in. In Italy, the Mafia hacked their way into one bank's computer network and diverted more than $100 million in European Union aid to Mob accounts."

MOB RULES

It's no surprise that the Sicilian Mafia was infiltrating profitable areas like wind and solar energy.
—Palermo magistrate Francesco Messineo, speaking
at a news conference

During a raid on Colombo don "Allie Boy" Persico's house, federal agents confiscated computer discs on which loan shark records were stored.

The Bonanno family hired an ultramodern hoodlum, "Tommy Computer," who regularly swept their social clubs for bugs.

Other hip mobsters joined the tech revolution, realized the profit potential, and went legit. They currently reside in oceanfront estates without the worry of losing their homes to the IRS.

New ideas appear every day, and new millionaires along with them. Smart mobsters stay on the cutting edge, and I don't mean by sharpening switchblades.

Keep up with the times.

LESSON 42

Flashiness Can End in the Flash of a Gun: Modesty

AL Capone and John Gotti both seized control of their respective crime families, wound up in front of cameras, loved the attention, and started to get flashy. Other mobsters laughed behind their backs; some tried to kill them, but Capone and Gotti both managed to die of natural causes. Other flashy mobsters haven't been so lucky.

Colombo capo William Cutolo was nicknamed "Wild Bill." America had a legendary gunfighter, Wild Bill Hickok. "Wild Bill" Cutolo believed he was also a legend and began to imitate the gunfighter by wearing cowboy boots, gaudy belt buckles, and ten-gallon hats. Sporting such attire in the middle of Bensonhurst is about as absurd as Clint Eastwood wearing a white Prada sweat suit, gold necklace, and diamond pinky ring in a spaghetti western.

Wild Bill exposed himself to the insults and ridicule of other mobsters, but he was a tough guy, a big earner, and the bosses liked him, so his antics were tolerated.

> Other mobsters didn't seem to like Legs [Diamond] much. Jealousy might have had something to do with it. He was the snappiest dressed mobster of the era. . . . He traveled around town by limousine, with an entourage of bodyguards that made him seem like a dignitary. And he almost always had a pretty dame on his arm.
> —T. J. English, *Paddy Whacked*

I met Wild Bill in a detention center while he was awaiting trial for murder and racketeering. Bill managed to stand out from other cons, with coiffed hair, manicured nails, and shiny shoes, the only ones I ever saw in prison. I still don't know where he got them.

Before Bill went on trial, another wiseguy told him, in a nice way, that if he happened to win, to count his blessings, accept that he didn't have many friends on the street because of his airs, and pack it in.

Bill was acquitted at trial. But he disregarded the other wiseguy's advice, and returned to the action on the streets of Brooklyn. Unfortunately, while Bill was away, his earning power had been reduced, as had the boss's patience for his arrogance and flamboyance.

On May 26, 1999, Bill slid into his Benz and was never seen again—until the FBI discovered his remains. Bill's killers may rattle off a dozen reasons why he died, and the FBI may have even more ideas. But the root of Bill's demise lies in the fact that nobody likes a flashy guy. First chance your enemies get, you're gone in a flash.

> The traditional mafioso . . . avoided any display of his own power that might provoke the envy of his rivals.
> —Pino Arlacchi, *Mafia Business*

If you're middle management, loud, arrogant, and full of pomp, your boss will put up with you as long as you're turning out the numbers. As soon as you're in a slump, you're gone.

Tone it down.

In the ancient world, Rome was warring with Carthage. The great Roman general Scipio Africanus took the fight to the enemy and defeated Carthage on its home turf.

Following his smashing victory, Scipio returned to Rome, where he was given a victory parade.

As Scipio rode along the parade route, Romans reached out to touch him, threw garlands, and blew kisses.

Scipio knew ahead of time that such attention would inflate his ego. To keep himself grounded, he appointed a slave to stand beside him in his chariot and whisper in his ear, "Remember, you're only a man."

Under the same circumstances, Wild Bill would've hired Bon Jovi to stand beside him in his chariot and sing, "I'm a cowboy, on a steel horse I ride . . ."

LESSON 43

Why a Mobster Makes His Son Pull the Trigger: Confidence Building

IN 1991, at the height of the Colombo War, Anthony Liberatore drove his son Chris to a Brooklyn bagel shop. Anthony waited in the car while Chris went into the shop and shot an eighteen-year-old worker twice in the face. The two imbeciles killed an innocent kid believing he was a member of the enemy faction.

As crazy as this sounds, a number of mobsters have brought their teenage sons along on a hit, sort of like Take Your Kid to Work Day. The idea is to break the son into The Life and build his confidence.

Nicer mobsters have a less violent approach to confidence building.

When I was young, a wiseguy took me to my first sit-down. Although I had no authority to speak at the table, he asked my opinion afterward. Here I was, a cub among lions, and he wanted to know what I thought.

For me, the confidence boost proved invaluable. What did he gain? The Mob's earning pyramid ensured that he'd benefit from my confidence.

Take your employees along to a big meeting. Ask their opinion afterward. Let them take the lead on a project. Trust them with more than they believe themselves capable of doing. It's how confidence is built. You and your company will be the immediate beneficiaries.

> It's chiefly to my confidence in men and my ability to inspire their confidence in me that I owe my success in life.
>
> —John D. Rockefeller, Sr.

A supervisor or manager should assess employees' potential, then push them outside their comfort zone. Trust them with more than they're currently responsible for.

Most employees will meet the challenge. In this manner, you strengthen employee confidence and benefit from their increased potential, like the wiseguy who brought me along to a sit. In time, I made the guy millions.

Just about everyone has heard of Alexander the Great, conqueror of the ancient world. Fewer people know about his father, King Philip II of Macedon.

When King Philip began to expand his empire, his greatest obstacle was Athens. To stem Philip's aggression, the Athenians led an army against him at the Battle of Chaeronea in August of 338 BCE.

Before the battle, Philip appointed his eighteen-year-old son, Alexander, to command the Macedonian cavalry. Not much was at stake, only life and death and the history of the world.

Would you gamble on a teen? My own father wouldn't lend me the keys to his car.

Philip's calculated risk paid off in spades. Young Alexander's cavalry played a major role in the Macedonian victory over Athens, and Philip's decision to entrust his son with more responsibility than the teen was used to proved instrumental in building Alexander's confidence.

When Philip died, Alexander took control of his army and became the youngest, greatest conqueror the world has ever known.

LESSON 44

Seize the Bull by the Horns—and Rip Off Its Balls:
The Fast and Decisive Leader

WHEN organized crime was beginning in America, the early god-fathers, vying for power, whacked each other left and right. After much bloodshed, Salvatore Maranzano emerged as king of the hill. Soon, one of his chief lieutenants, "Lucky" Luciano, decided to knock him off. But icing Maranzano proved to be a challenge since he had a full-time personal guard.

When Luciano heard that Maranzano had tax problems and expected a visit from the IRS, Luciano hatched a plan and executed it in no time. He sent his crew of Young Turks to Maranzano's office, posing as IRS agents. After flashing phony badges to gain entry, Luciano's men drew weapons on Maranzano, and his audit became an autopsy.

Luciano had seized the bull by the horns—and ripped off its balls.

A few decades later, the American Mafia had matured, but the need to act quickly and decisively remained just as critical. Colombo mobster "Crazy Joey" Gallo killed a lot of men, and was marked for death by his own crime family. But no one could get near him. Even if someone could, Gallo was always accompanied by a tough bodyguard, "Pete the Greek" Diapoulas.

Gallo liked the Hollywood scene and hung out with entertainers. After a night of partying with a few movie stars, including Jerry Orbach of *Law & Order* fame, Gallo and Pete the Greek went to a late dinner at a restaurant in Manhattan's Little Italy.

Gallo ate, drank, and laughed, unaware he'd been spotted by a low-level thug trying to make his bones with the Colombo family.

The thug ran up the block to a Chinese take-out joint where four Colombo mobsters were eating, and told them he'd just spotted Gallo.

In a hot second, the mobsters dropped their egg rolls, picked up their guns, and phoned their capo, who said, "Get Gallo!"

Within minutes, they went from Moo Goo Gai Pan to Joe Gallo Dead Man.

Like Luciano and his crew, the Colombo mobsters seized the moment, knowing an opportunity might not present itself again.

In the cutthroat world of business, it's necessary to act quickly and decisively, and take out the competition in the process.

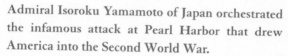

Admiral Isoroku Yamamoto of Japan orchestrated the infamous attack at Pearl Harbor that drew America into the Second World War.

During the war, the Americans broke the Japanese naval code and discovered that Yamamoto was planning a flight over the South Pacific.

American fighter pilots immediately requested permission to take out the Japanese admiral and were told, "Get Yamamoto!"

With little time to plan, the Americans equipped their P-38 fighters with extra fuel tanks for the long-range flight and took to the sky.

Right on time, they ambushed Yamamoto's large escort squadron, zeroing in on Yamamoto's plane. Admiral Matome Ugaki, a witness to the American pilots' resolve, said, "They bore down mercilessly."

Later, a Japanese search party located Yamamoto in the jungle. He'd been thrown from his plane, still strapped into his seat and gripping his samurai sword, two bullets inside him. The hit went down without a hitch.

The Americans acted quickly and decisively, and seized the bull by the horns, like Luciano, who took out Maranzano, and the Colombo mobsters who knocked off Gallo.

LESSON 45

Just Get the Job Done!: Flexibility

MY crew and I were in the middle of a heist when the employees told us that the particular employee entrusted with the combination to the safe was on vacation. The safe was too big to carry, so I started calling around, asking if anyone could get me a safecracker right away.

A friend connected me with Vinnie the Vault. Vinnie asked for 30 percent of the take. I thought it was steep but I had no choice; I was too far into the job to walk away. I told Vinnie where we were, and he showed up about twenty minutes later with a sledgehammer and a tool bag.

"What the fuck is this?" I asked. Naturally, I'd expected the guy to pull on some leather gloves, put a stethoscope to the safe, and spin the dial.

"It's my safecracking equipment," he replied. "I can open any safe."

Vinnie opened his tool bag and went to work. He drilled and banged away at the safe until sheets of metal peeled back, concrete crumbled, and steel mesh appeared. Using giant clippers, Vinnie cut the mesh, banged some more, and we were in.

We cleaned out the safe, gave the putz his 30 percent, and left.

Handing Vinnie his end, I felt like I'd been taken by a con man. Imagine that—robbing something from someone else and then getting annoyed that someone else is robbing some of it from me? Then I thought, Hey, he got the job done, and that's the bottom line. How he did it really wasn't my business.

> Humphreys gets the job done, and he gets it done smart.
> —Sam Giancana, praising gangster Murray "The Camel" Humphreys

MOB RULES

A lot of people expect things done a certain way and fail to realize that everyone has their own way of doing things. Let them do their thing. As long as they get the job done, mind your own business.

Catherine de' Medici was a Mafia princess if ever there was one.

The men in her family have been referred to as "godfathers of the Renaissance." Like Mob bosses, they controlled Florence through murder, bribery, and intrigue.

For political reasons, the pope arranged a marriage between Catherine de' Medici and Henry, Prince of France (later King Henry II). To keep the marriage binding, Catherine needed to produce an heir to the throne.

Before the age of Viagra, Henry was having trouble pulling this off. The pope grew frustrated with the situation and said to Catherine, "A clever girl surely knows how to get pregnant somehow or other."

In other words, just get the job done.

LESSON 46

We Shot Him Twelve Times and He Lived:
Most Problems Take Care of Themselves

LUCCHESE underboss Anthony "Gaspipe" Casso, suspecting wiseguy "Fat Pete" Chiodo of going sour, ordered a hit team to take him down.

After stalking Chiodo, the hit men ambushed him at a Staten Island gas station, while Chiodo was checking his oil. They hit Chiodo with a hail of gunfire but he survived—his layers of fat served as a bulletproof vest, absorbing the lead.

I knew a couple of Chiodo's would-be assassins, some of the funniest guys I've ever met. When joking about the hit, one of them told me, "We shot him twelve fuckin' times an' he lived. Before we shot him, he could barely breathe. Now, he's got a team of nurses monitoring his health around the clock. He's even got a dietitian; he's never been healthier in his life. An' he owes it all to us. Had we left him alone, he'd have dropped dead on his own."

Everyone involved on the hit attempt went to prison because of it.

Contrary to what the paranoid Casso believed when he ordered the hit on Chiodo, Chiodo was no snitch—that is, until after he was shot. Once Chiodo had been betrayed by his friends, he felt no qualms about becoming an FBI informant.

As the hit men who joked with me had realized, it's sometimes best to leave well enough alone.

Learn to distinguish between real problems that need attention and those that are inconsequential, many of which take care of themselves.

LESSON 47

Aye, You Know Who My Uncle Is?: Everyone Is Important

IN Brooklyn and Queens, just about everyone is connected somehow. Being in The Life, you're aware of this fact and treat everyone with respect—just in case.

> Everyone I know in the New York area has brushed up against the American Mafia at one time or another.
>
> —Selwyn Raab, *Five Families*

John Gotti's first highly publicized indictment after becoming boss of the Gambino family was a minor assault case that stemmed from a parking incident.

Some legitimate guy picked a fight with Gotti and Gotti kicked his ass. Typical of your average wiseass who starts a fight and then loses, the guy went crying to the police. Gotti got picked up for assault, and that's when the guy found out whom he'd fucked with. The case went to trial and, after the guy got amnesia on the witness stand, Gotti was acquitted.

The guy was lucky to walk away with his life, and learned to respect people the hard way.

Mob informant Sammy "The Bull" Gravano was always a weasel. Yet he was able to shoot and bullshit his way to the top of the Gambino family. Certain wiseguys who knew Sammy before he was a big shot pegged him as a petty, devious sneak, but discounted him because of these frailties. And those who treated him poorly on his way to the top of the Mob ladder paid with their lives once he got there.

When Sammy defected to the government, he came up with creative stories for why he had killed people, usually blaming his later murders on his boss, John Gotti, using the classic Nuremberg defense: "I was only following orders."

One such murder Sammy orchestrated was that of Gambino soldier Louis DiBono. Sammy blamed Gotti for the murder, but in truth DiBono died because he pissed Sammy off when Sammy was still a nobody.

DiBono's death presents a perfect example of why you must treat everyone with respect, even when they're not important. When DiBono disrespected the young Gravano, he never could have imagined the twist of fate that would one day catapult Sammy into power.

Here's how it happened:

Early in his career, Sammy latched on to Brooklyn wiseguy Frankie DeCicco. When Queens wiseguy John Gotti wanted to kill his don, Paul Castellano, he needed to build a Brooklyn alliance to keep the family intact. Gotti, the consummate politician, confided his plan to DeCicco, who signed on.

Gotti and DeCicco planned to share power if the coup succeeded, which it did.

After Castellano was dead, DeCicco became Gotti's underboss, and Sammy, being close with DeCicco, moved up a notch.

The wheel of fate was not done spinning.

When rival mobsters tried to kill Gotti with a car bomb, they missed their target and blew up DeCicco instead.

Now that DeCicco was dead, Gotti had to appoint a new underboss from Brooklyn since the Brooklynites had been promised a role in the new regime. Due to Sammy's proximity to DeCicco, Gotti chose Sammy to fill DeCicco's blown-up shoes.

Now tell me, could DiBono have imagined all this when he disrespected Sammy "The Nobody" years before? Well, he has eternity to think about it.

Once in power, Sammy "The Grudge" conjured up a reason to have DiBono whacked. DiBono's 350-pound body was found stuffed in a car trunk in the basement of the World Trade Center. (As further testament to Mob business savvy, DiBono had secured a legit multimillion-dollar contract to fireproof the steel supports of the Twin Towers, and that's where his killers ambushed him.)

Today, DiBono would tell you to think twice about those nitwits in your office who you're just certain will never amount to anything. You never know where someone will be tomorrow.

Treat everyone with respect.

In February of 1930, Chicago mobster "Machine Gun" Jack McGurn was pulled over by police for speeding. Sitting beside McGurn was a young man.

The cop, who knew McGurn, asked him, "Who's this new punk?"

McGurn answered, "He's no punk. He's a solid fella. This boy is going places."

"What's his name?" asked the cop.

"Tony Accardo."

Tony "Joe Batters" Accardo would succeed Al Capone and rule Chicago for nearly five decades. He ordered the deaths of more than two hundred people, controlled Las Vegas, the Teamsters' billion-dollar fund, and Chicago's police force and politicians. Some punk.

Around the same time McGurn and Accardo were speeding around Chicago, Michael Collins and Eamon de Valera were vying for control of an Irish revolutionary movement that amounted to little more than a mob: stealing, violence, and gunning down informants.

With only room for one at the top, the cunning de Valera set up Collins to look like a traitor, then had him whacked. In typical Mob fashion, Collins bought it with a dum-dum bullet to the head.

De Valera was now undisputed boss of the Irish mob, or revolutionary movement.

About six years before de Valera iced Collins, he and some of his gang were convicted of treason and scheduled to be executed by the British government. For political reasons, the Brits decided to commute some of the sentences. The executioner, Sir John Maxwell, received news from Britain to halt the executions.

"Who's next on the list?" asked Maxwell.

"Connolly," answered an underling.

"We can't let him off," said Maxwell. "Who's next?"

"De Valera."

"Is he someone important?" asked Maxwell.

"No, just a schoolteacher."

"All right," said Maxwell. "Go ahead with Connolly and stop with this fellow."

Like Tony "Joe Batters" Accardo, who went on to control Chicago for nearly fifty years after being called a "punk," Eamon de Valera controlled Ireland for nearly fifty years after being referred to as "just a schoolteacher."

You never know who you're talking to. Treat everyone with respect.

LESSON 48

What Am I, a Gavone?:
What People Really Think About You

SURE, plenty of mobsters are insecure or vain, constantly worrying about their image. But I knew one wiseguy who paid close attention to his image, and was neither vain nor insecure. Just smart.

I attended a few meetings on the street with a wiseguy I'll call Philly Blake. We once left a meeting and Philly asked, "What do they think about me?"

"Who gives a shit?" I replied.

The next time we left a meeting, Philly asked me that same question and I rolled my eyes. Philly shook his head.

"You don't understand," he said. "It's important to see yourself the way others do." When Philly put it in those terms, it didn't seem like such a ridiculous question after all.

> The eye sees not itself.
> —Brutus, in Shakespeare's *Julius Caesar*

Ever wonder how you appear through the eyes of other people? It's worth pondering every now and then. Who am I? How do I conduct myself? Am I gruff or polite? Cheap or charitable? Can I be counted on? Am I the guy you'd want your daughter to marry? What defines me? And what do others say and think about me when my name comes up?

> The unexamined life is not worth living.
> —Socrates

The first words inscribed on the wall inside the ancient Temple of Apollo at Delphi were "Know thyself." A simple, brilliant phrase. How many of us really know ourselves?

The ancient Greeks also said, "Character is destiny." If so, can we use Philly Blake's advice to analyze ourselves and change our character, and in turn, alter our destiny?

LESSON 49

Play the Fence and You're Sure to Fall Off

THE Mafia's first major war in America was the Castellammarese War, which lasted from 1929 to 1931. This bloody conflict, fought for control of the American Mafia, was waged between the forces of Joe "The Boss" Masseria and Salvatore Maranzano.

As many as a hundred mobsters may have been killed during the war. Internal tension led to backstabbing, and splinter factions on both sides emerged.

One wiseguy stood out among the many who changed sides as tides turned: Anthony "Tony Bender" Strollo. Tony Bender was involved in the rackets from an early age. When the Castellammarese War broke out, he aligned with Masseria. When Masseria's ship looked in danger of sinking, Tony Bender dove overboard into Maranzano's ship. And when Maranzano's crew mutinied, he threw in with the mutineers. The Fletcher Christian of this gang of mutineers was Charles "Lucky" Luciano.

> [Tony Bender] was pretty good at workin' both sides of the street an' gettin' away with it.
>
> —Lucky Luciano

The war ended and Bender was employed for a while under Luciano.

When Luciano went to prison, Bender picked up with a new boss, Vito Genovese.

When Genovese fled to Italy to avoid a murder rap, Bender latched on to another boss, Frank Costello, who had never particularly cared for Genovese.

When Genovese had Costello shot, Bender went back with Genovese.

When Genovese was sent to prison, Bender pledged his loyalty to the boss of yet another family, Carlo Gambino.

By then, the Mob was finally fed up with Tony Bender's bullshit. He went missing and his body has never been found.

When you play the fence, you're sure to fall off. Had Bender studied history, he might have avoided his dreadful end.

When war broke out between Sparta and Athens, the young Alcibiades fought for Athens. Peace was made but war between these two states broke out again.

This time, Alcibiades jumped ship and went over to Sparta.

In time, Alcibiades fled Sparta and made his way over to Persia, a third power that hated the other two.

With a lot of Persian money, and maybe a few rugs, Alcibiades returned to Athens and conned the Athenians into accepting him back—just as Genovese was conned into accepting Bender back after he'd aligned himself with Costello, Genovese's enemy.

Yet again, Alcibiades abandoned his latest allegiance, went back to Persia, and became a counselor to the Persian king. At last, in Persia, Alcibiades bit the dust, just like Tony Bender, who became a counselor to Don Carlo Gambino as his final move before getting whacked.

Backstabbing. Shifting alliances. A man's luck runs out. This exact drama has played out throughout human history. Don't be the next idiot to accept the lead role.

Play the fence and you're sure to fall off.

LESSON 50

Italians Talk with Their Hands: Body Language

SOME schmo accidentally hit a boy with his car. The boy was fine, minor scrapes and bruises, but the kid's father, a knock-around guy, went berserk. I knew the father, and knew he was serious when he vowed to kill the driver.

When the driver got wind that he was in trouble with a knock-around guy, he went to a local hoodlum, Greedy Pete, and asked for his help. Pete knew I was friendly with the kid's father and came to me. Not to save the driver's life, but to put the squeeze on him. (Be careful who you turn to in a time of need.)

"He's loaded," Pete said to me. "Let's milk him dry."

Pete's plan was to turn the heat up on the driver and frighten him even more, but assure him he could buy his way out of the problem. My job was to calm the kid's father and promise him a cash reward for scrapping his murderous plan.

Over the next week, Pete met with the driver on several occasions. Between meetings, he pretended to go back and forth with the boy's angry father in an effort to negotiate a settlement. In truth, Pete was reporting to me.

At first, the driver offered ten grand to bury the incident and save his own life. Pete's goal was to bring the settlement up to fifty large. At every five-thousand-dollar hike, the driver claimed he couldn't go for another nickel. But each time he lied, and later agreed to cough up more until finally, at thirty-five grand, Pete came to me and said, "He's done. We can't squeeze him for another penny."

I found this hard to believe. The driver had lied all week. Why believe him now? Was Greedy Pete bullshitting me, skimming fifteen off the top for himself?

"Lou," Pete said to me. "I'm doin' this a long time. I know when a guy's bullshittin', an' when he's not. If we push him any harder, he'll either drive himself to the police station or off the edge of a cliff."

"How'd you know he was bullshittin' all week, but he ain't now?"

"I don't go by words," said Pete. "Everyone lies. I go by eyes, hands, breathin', an' every other fuckin' thing."

I accepted Pete's reasoning—for the very same reasons—and we settled for thirty-five G's. I'd like to say we gave it to the boy for his college fund. Instead, we took ten grand apiece, me, Pete, and the father, and kicked five upstairs.

Almost all people use body language. They may not talk with their hands—like many Italians—but they give up clues in a million different ways that either confirm or betray their words. Being aware of these clues gives you the edge in any negotiation.

> The tongue was given [to] the diplomat so that he could conceal his thoughts.
> —Talleyrand, foreign minister and consigliere to Napoleon

In the Mob, body language can be used to gauge how much someone is willing to pay for a stolen load, whether a guy has your money when he claims he doesn't, or how heavy you can lean on a guy before he looks for another way out. The examples are endless and can be applied daily in the business world.

Don't trust words if the body is saying something different.

LESSON 51

Deliver the Goods: Stand Behind Your Name

WHEN Philly mobster Nicholas "Nick the Blade" Virgilio was indicted for murder, he met with a crooked municipal court judge named Edwin Helfant. Helfant claimed to have a relationship with Virgilio's sentencing judge, and offered to fix Virgilio's sentence for twelve grand.

Virgilio forked over the money—and got slammed in court anyhow.

Six years later, Virgilio was released from jail early on account of good behavior. He began to stalk Helfant. One snowy day, Virgilio bought a shovel, ski mask, gloves, and a .22-caliber pistol. Posing as a snow shoveler in need of the men's room, Virgilio walked into a lounge where Helfant was dining with his wife. When Virgilio left the lounge, Helfant was slumped over in his seat, dead.

There is a certain honor among thieves, and the Mob firmly believes that everyone should get what they pay for.

> A handshake from Meyer Lansky was worth more than the strongest contracts that a battery of lawyers could put together.
> —Ralph Salerno, retired NYPD Mob investigator

How many calls are dropped on your mobile phone each month? And yet the phone company demands its bill. How many products have you purchased this year that broke on account of poor manufacturing? Don't you love those limited warranties that cover every possible problem but the one that's bound to happen? Do you like talking to an automated recording when you need a live customer service rep? How about waiting twenty or thirty minutes on hold to get through to that rep, then getting disconnected, and having to start all over again? Does anyone stand behind their service or product pledge?

If you're paid for a service or a product, deliver!

> No one had any problem dealing with a kid. My word was good. I delivered.
>
> —*Unlocked*

Don't take people's money, jerk them off, and go have a drink in a lounge, like Edwin Helfant. Stand behind your name. When it comes down to it, it's all you've got.

LESSON 52

Fireproof Your Ass:
Never Let Anyone Light a Flame Under You

AT one time, a pair of con men in Queens would drive around in a van on the lookout for an average Joe, usually a guy at a gas station or walking along the sidewalk. Once the crooks spotted their target, the van would screech to a halt and the side door would slide open. One crook would jump out and point to a stack of TV boxes inside the van.

"We just knocked off this joint," he'd say. "Gotta move fast, thirty-two-inch TVs. Want one?"

Understand that Queens isn't Beverly Hills; most residents in the low-income neighborhoods are acquainted with crime and unfazed by a situation like this. Blue-collar workers can always use a discount, and most don't feel that buying a hot item is the same as committing a crime. Think of the millions of people who buy bootleg DVDs.

If the guy told the crooks, "I'm not interested," they'd speed away, on to the next sucker.

If the guy hesitated, the crooks would know he was ripe for their con, and step up the pressure.

"C'mon, buddy, make up your mind," one might say. "I gotta dump this stuff."

The one driving the van might yell "Hurry up!" or rev the engine to force a decision.

The guy had no time to ask questions—or open a box to check the merchandise.

"How much?" is all the crooks would need to hear to know they'd hooked a fish.

They might ask for a hundred bucks, but they'd take whatever the guy was willing to pay. If the guy scraped together fifty bucks, they'd say, "Okay, but only because I gotta move fast."

When the guy got home and opened the box, he'd find a few bricks wrapped in newspaper.

These crooks succeeded because they were experts at rushing people into making on-the-spot decisions. They'd catch their prey off-guard when their van screeched to a halt. Once they knew they had a possible sale, they'd step up the pressure.

Any guy afraid to walk away from a "great" deal that seems to have fallen into his lap is ripe for a con.

> [N]ever give an immediate reply to any proposition . . . nor to any complaint or unexpected offer. . . . One must always have time to reflect, and it is better to put off to tomorrow what one cannot do readily and well today, than to act precipitously.
>
> —Talleyrand

There are plenty of crooks in the business world who might try to rush you into a decision. It's okay to stall people who put pressure on you, because it probably means they're bullshitting you. If not, they'll respect your need to think things through.

LESSON 53

Go to Bat for Your Guys: Loyalty to Your Employees

BONANNO hit man Louie Tuzzio popped Gus Farace in response to Farace's reckless murder of DEA agent Everett Hatcher. When Tuzzio ambushed Farace, there was a passenger in Farace's car who also got hit by the shots. The passenger was the son of a Gambino soldier. Although the soldier's son made a full recovery, the soldier asked his don, John Gotti, for street justice; he wanted the hit man, Louie Tuzzio, killed.

Contrary to media tags at the time, Gotti was no boss of bosses. Although he ruled his own family, he had no authority over wiseguys in other families. Bonanno family acting boss Anthony Spero was the man responsible for Tuzzio. All Gotti could do was approach Spero and request that Tuzzio be killed for his mistake.

Spero did not have to answer to Gotti. He had a choice. He could deny the request and go to bat for his own guy, or pop Tuzzio and ingratiate himself with Gotti. While Spero may have agonized over the decision to kill Tuzzio, in the end, he had him killed.

John Gotti was placed in the same exact predicament as Spero when a member of Gotti's *borgata* put out a contract on Lucchese underboss Anthony "Gaspipe" Casso. Casso was injured but survived the hit. After Casso recovered, he tracked down the hit man who shot him, and tortured the man until he gave up the wiseguy who'd dispatched him. The wiseguy, Angelo Ruggiero, was a member of Gotti's personal crew.

Casso went to Gotti and asked that Ruggiero be put to sleep. At the time, Gotti's power was new and insecure. He'd recently usurped the Gambino throne and was trying to build alliances with other families. In short, Gotti needed friends, not enemies.

From a strictly political standpoint, Gotti should have sacrificed Ruggiero. Wouldn't Machiavelli himself have advised Gotti to do so? But Gotti refused, incurring Casso's wrath and that of the Lucchese family.

Gotti knew politics better than anyone, but wasn't about to sell out his own guys.

> These settlers may have owed their wealth to commerce, or to agriculture, or to the increase in their population, or *perhaps to the moral integrity which prompted them to stand by their allies until they themselves were destroyed*; at any rate, as I said, they quickly grew prosperous.
>
> —Livy, *A History of Rome*

In the movie *The Untouchables,* there's a scene in which Al Capone, played by Robert De Niro, bludgeons two men to death with a baseball bat. The scene was factual. Capone did kill the two men, Anselmi and Scalise, after he found out they had conspired to kill him.

A few years before Capone killed Anselmi and Scalise, he was asked to hand them over to Hymie Weiss, a gangster Capone was warring with at the time. Weiss, who had a personal vendetta against Anselmi and Scalise, promised to end the fighting with Capone after the two men were handed over for execution. Capone wanted the fighting to stop so he could resume business without interference.

> It's in the DNA of Cosa Nostra to avoid any internal clash because it would mean an opportunity for the police to investigate and fight them.
>
> —Col. Mauro Obinu, carabinieri

Still, he refused. "I wouldn't do that to a yellow dog!" was Capone's unequivocal response to Weiss's request.

Al Capone and John Gotti had many character flaws, but they were loyal to their men. Even Casso, who tried to kill Gotti, had to admit, "[Gotti's] one of the few people whose word you could take to the bank."

Go to bat for your people.

LESSON 54

Rest in Peace—in a Lakeside Cabin, Not an Early Grave: Taking a Break and Coming Back Refreshed

IN the 1990s, I knew a mobster who owned a string of successful businesses. He was a workaholic, incapable of taking a break. He once planned a two-week vacation to Florida. After two days, he called the office and said, "I'm on the next flight home." He was back to work before the day was up.

He was obviously married to his business, not his wife. As a result, his marriage ended in divorce. Unable to keep up the hectic pace, he began to use prescription drugs and eventually crashed, losing everything he'd worked so hard to gain.

The human mind and body can run like a race car, but they can't sustain high speeds without a pit stop. There's a fine line between hard work and overwork. That's why smart mobsters take a break from the action.

Genovese boss Anthony "Fat Tony" Salerno kept a farm in Rhinebeck, New York. Colombo boss Carmine Persico escaped to his estate in Saugerties, New York, and Gambino boss John Gotti had a summer home in Pennsylvania. The list of mobsters who retreated to homes far away from the action is endless. But you don't always have to go far to get away. Bonanno wiseguy Anthony Spero raised homing pigeons on his roof in Brooklyn, as did Dominick Napolitano and other prominent wiseguys.

After the stress of a big score, I'd personally take off for the Poconos or head out to Long Island for a long walk on the beach. A couple of days of R and R and I'd return to the streets refreshed and eager for business.

A cabin getaway can provide you with the perfect antidote for stress, a million times better than drugs or, worse, a psychiatrist, some of whom are more nuts than anybody. While tucked away in that cabin, clear your mind. If your mind wanders back to the office, control your thoughts, don't let them control you.

One of the Ten Commandments tells us to keep a day of complete rest, a Sabbath.

A mobster may break every other commandment but he'll keep a little Sabbath of his own, and return to the streets a new man.

LESSON 55

Don't Split Yourself in Half:
The Wrong Decision Is Better Than None at All

ON April 16, 1984, cops in Garfield, New Jersey, answered a call at a warehouse where they found two fifty-gallon drums filled with body parts. Inside one drum was a man's head and torso. Inside the other, his legs. It took three months for forensic technicians to identify the grisly remains as those of Cesare Bonventre.

Bonventre was a thirty-three-year-old wiseguy with the Bonanno family when he was murdered. The family was involved in a power struggle, and Bonventre was cut in half while in the process of deciding to whom he would swear allegiance.

A wrong decision is better than none at all. An error can be fixed, and you've got a shot at getting it right. No decision will get you nowhere.

Dictator Benito Mussolini ruled Italy like a Mafia don. So much so that he launched a crusade against Italy's real Mafia dons, regarding them as a threat to his power.

In 1922, Mussolini used his talent for resolute decision making when he and his gang marched on Rome and seized power from an impotent king and a horde of disorganized politicians. But in 1939, at the start of World War II, Mussolini made a critical blunder by choosing to fight alongside Nazi Germany instead of the Allies.

Six years later, with Italy in ruins, Mussolini's son Vittorio asked him how he had fucked up so badly in aligning Italy with the Nazis.

In so many words, Mussolini told Vittorio that he'd simply picked the wrong horse. The decision was based on many complex factors, but Mussolini was a practical man and knew, in the end, that it came down to that.

However wrong Mussolini's decisions were, he reached the heights of power by making decisions. Unlike Bonventre, who was cut in half, halfway up the career ladder.

LESSON 56

New Orleans Wasn't Built in a Day

FOR decades, Carlos Marcello was the undisputed Mafia boss of Louisiana.

Marcello's capacity to both think ahead and move one step at a time was evident even in his early years. As a boy, the future don was so poor, he couldn't even afford a gun. He came up with the idea of borrowing one to stick up a grocery store. He'd then use the loot from the grocery store stickup to purchase two more guns. With three guns, Marcello and his gang of youths would have enough firepower to hold up a bank and make off with a bundle.

Granted, we're not talking about pulling off the Pink Panther jewel heist here, but Marcello showed an early ability to plan several moves in advance.

Marcello went from sticking up a grocery store, to owning a dive lounge, to running a casino, to dominating the underworld. Using the same methodical approach as a legit businessman—acquire capital, invest wisely, spend money to make money—he eventually owned restaurants, motels, marinas, banks and bars, gas stations, cab companies, and a fleet of shrimp boats.

Some of these businesses were started with Mafia money, but that doesn't diminish the credit Marcello deserves for making them successful. If one man invests from his dishonest dealings, another from his family's coffers, yet another obtains a business grant or low-interest bank loan, all three men start off on an equal footing, except that the mobster's acquisition of funds was accompanied by a wealth of experiences. A bank or personal loan offers nothing valuable besides the money.

Many of the legit businesses Marcello started in Louisiana decades ago are still in operation today. Like a talented chess player,

Marcello planned several moves in advance, but always moved one piece at a time. In this manner, he entered the game of life a pawn and left it a king.

If you plan to build an empire, realize, as Marcello did, that the greatest accomplishments are the sum of numerous short-term achievements, carried out with an eye on the big prize.

LESSON 57

Bugsy and Bacchus: The Lessons of History

FLORIDA Mob boss Santo Trafficante was a voracious reader of histories and biographies. Carlo Gambino quoted Machiavelli, and Joe Bonanno read classics from Homer to Dante. These three Mafia bosses were titans of organized crime, and applied learned wisdom to everyday problems, and imparted that wisdom to underlings. Anyone familiar with their lives will conclude that reading was undoubtedly connected with their success.

> Mr. and Mrs. Santo Trafficante stay around the house at all times . . . and all they ever do is read books.
> —Trafficante housemaid, responding to FBI questioning

Jewish mobsters Bugsy Siegel and Meyer Lansky grew up together on the streets of New York. As boys, they shared the same aspirations, chose the same career path, and proved to be equally cold and calculating. As adults, their business lives were very similar, but their hobbies were different.

Lansky was an avid reader, a loyal member of the Book-of-the-Month Club. He'd usually tuck into bed early with a good read.

> I had a great desire for learning.
> —Meyer Lansky

Siegel, on the other hand, had no time for books. He liked fast money and fast cars, and wheeled and dealed recklessly. His major deal was turning a small town in the Mojave Desert into a playground for joy seekers. Using investors' funds, he built his dream hotel and casino, the Flamingo, in Las Vegas.

When Siegel's hotel wasn't finished on time and construction went way over budget, his Mafia investors concluded that he was embezzling the dough. They also ridiculed Siegel for falling in love with a former prostitute, Virginia Hill. The Mob believed that Hill was manipulating Siegel and squirreling away a small fortune, derived from their investments.

Had Siegel, like Lansky, studied history, he'd have known of Pericles, the famous Athenian statesman and city planner, who had been involved in a large construction project called the Parthenon. Pericles also used investors' dough to build the Parthenon. When construction went way over budget, his Athenian investors concluded that Pericles was embezzling the dough. They also ridiculed Pericles for falling in love with a former prostitute, Aspasia. Aspasia, like Hill, used Pericles' power and connections to squirrel away a fortune.

> Aspasia . . . what great art of power this woman had, that she managed as she pleased the foremost men of the state.
>
> —Plutarch, *Life of Pericles*

> Virginia Hill also managed as she pleased the foremost men of the Mafia, including Frank Costello, Frank Nitti, Joe Adonis, Tony Accardo, and Murray "The Camel" Humphreys.

Here lies the wisdom of history: Pericles and Siegel. Identical circumstances. Two thousand years apart.

Had Siegel read history, as did Lansky, Gambino, Bonanno, and Trafficante, he might have avoided the same pitfalls as Pericles, and died in bed of natural causes, like the Mob bosses just mentioned above. Instead, Siegel's angry investors had him whacked.

Siegel was lounging on a couch at Hill's house on the night he was riddled with bullets. His right eye was blown out of his head and landed fifteen feet from his body. It's said that one of the bullets fired at Siegel "shattered a small marble figure of Bacchus that stood on Virginia Hill's piano."

Bacchus, the ancient god of wine and intoxication, is commonly associated with nightlife. His statue was gunned down alongside Siegel. The ancients would have adopted this curious coincidence as the perfect storyline for a cautionary tale.

Though Siegel's death could have been avoided, he paid a posthumous tribute to Pericles. Today there is a Parthenon Convention Center in Las Vegas, the nightlife mecca of the world.

The achievements of two dreamers who made the same mistakes are fused forever in the Mojave Desert.

LESSON 58

Time to Go: How to Leave the Organization

WHEN I decided to leave the Mob, I approached each of the bosses I was in prison with at the time and told them I wanted to take up a new path. I was careful not to insult The Life, I just told them the truth: that it was no longer for me. Aside from the obvious moral reasons one would walk away from crime, it was fair to say that with all the snitches leading us to jail, the Mob wasn't offering much room for advancement.

Each boss I spoke with knew I never snitched on anyone, had no outstanding debts, and had upheld the integrity of the organization. They wished me luck. Some bosses continued to seek my advice with regard to problems in their families, immediate and extended. I offered my opinions, careful not to entangle myself in any new conspiracies.

Today, I bump into a mobster from the old days every now and then; I keep it friendly and encounter no animosity or bitterness.

There may come a time when you'll face a similar situation. You've been leading people for a while. You've acquired enough knowledge and wisdom to run the company on your own and may indeed be doing just that, but without the benefits. Are you content to stay where you are, or is it time to move on?

First, you have to assess your possibilities for advancement inside the company. If it looks grim and you plan to walk, do it with tact. Don't make enemies.

If you've adhered to the advice I've given thus far, then you've earned for the company, haven't snitched on anyone, never embarrassed anyone in public, and mentored employees in private. You've tempered your firmness with mercy, and allowed people a chance to be imperfect, or human. If you've handled yourself with integrity, you shouldn't have a problem moving on.

Your coworkers will be sad to see you go, but will respect your decision and wish you well. Some employees may follow you wherever you go. Your old bosses, like mine, may even continue to seek your advice.

Whether you become the don of your own company or the don of the company you now work for, apply what you've learned, and you'll prosper.

Lots of luck, whatever you decide.

PART III

LESSONS FOR A DON (BOSS)

[A don] must possess a rare combination of traits. Like the CEO of a large corporation, or the commanding general of an army, he must be courageous, aggressive, energetic, shrewd, resourceful, intelligent, and have the ability to inspire unquestioning loyalty in his subordinates. . . . He must be an administrator, a judge, a politician, a diplomat, a general, [and] a businessman.

—John H. Davis, *Mafia Dynasty*

LESSON 59

You Gotta Know When to Fold 'em: Controlling Your Ambition

CARLO Gambino was arguably the most successful American Mafia don ever. In 1957, he succeeded Albert "The Mad Hatter" Anastasia as boss of a vicious family dubbed Murder, Inc., and molded it into Money, Inc., the most lucrative family in the country during his lifetime.

Gambino introduced a number of new rackets. He secured the docks, took over the longshoremen's union, supplied construction materials for skyscrapers, and provided poultry for restaurants and supermarkets. These new rackets lined the pockets of nearly everyone in the family.

Like old world royalty, Gambino arranged the marriage of his son to the daughter of another Mafia don, creating an alliance that allowed his crime family entry into the Garment District, various labor unions, and the trucking industry. Gambino built an army of more than a thousand soldiers, and expanded the family's network across the country.

These revolutionary initiatives suggest that Gambino was a man ruled by unbridled ambition. But if you study his life carefully, you'll find that he was able to regulate his ambition according to circumstances.

(This is no easy task. Ask Ken Lay and Jeff Skilling, the makers and breakers of Enron, how hard it is to control one's ambitions.)

> Human strength is not in extremes, but in avoiding extremes.
>
> —Ralph Waldo Emerson

After a lifetime of progress, Gambino noticed that times had changed. Newer wiseguys disregarded rules and destroyed families by selling drugs. Many were flashy and loud, instead of low-key and respectful. Gambino grew wary of expansion and warned future Mafia leaders to exercise moderation. He ultimately "closed the books" to his family (i.e., no new employees), and then withdrew to his Long Island home, where he died peacefully while watching a Yankees game at the age of seventy-four.

> [Don Angelo] Bruno wielded power, but also recognized that with that power came responsibility . . . he knew his limits. He knew when to push and when to pull back.
> —George Anastasia, *Blood and Honor*

A mere ten years after Gambino died, his nightmare vision of the family's future was realized in a thuggish, glitzy, drug-dealing don named John Gotti, the polar opposite of Gambino. In many ways, Gotti was just as sharp as Gambino, but cut from a very different cloth.

How was Gambino able to predict the future? By looking back at the past.

Gambino was a student of Italian history. He often quoted Machiavelli and emulated the leadership qualities of the better Roman emperors.

> I'll have to hand it to Napoleon as the world's greatest racketeer. But I could have wised him up on some things . . . he overplayed his hand . . . he was just like the rest of us. He didn't know when to quit and had to get back in the racket.
> —Al Capone comments after reading Emil Ludwig's *Napoleon*

Augustus Caesar was arguably the most successful of all Roman emperors. Augustus succeeded Julius Caesar after he was brutally murdered—just as Gambino succeeded Albert Anastasia after he was murdered.

Augustus was driven by ambition, hell-bent on expansion. He built road networks that enlarged the empire's boundaries, and started a police force, a fire department, and a courier system similar to our post office. He also orchestrated marriage alliances for economic and political purposes, as did Gambino.

Toward the end of his life, Augustus noticed that times had changed and grew wary of expansion. He warned future Roman emperors to exercise moderation. And died peacefully at the age of seventy-six.

Both Augustus and Gambino knew when to throttle down their ambitions.

Running an empire, a Mafia family, or a business is like driving a car. You've got to know when to hit the gas, and when to brake.

> Sir, if there is one thing above all others a successful man should know, it is *when to stop.*
>
> —Coenus to Alexander the Great

LESSON 60

It's Strictly Business: Friends or Enemies?

SAYING no to a friend can be the hardest thing to do—but in the Mob, it's almost always your best friend who kills you. Sometimes, he sets you up. Other times, he pulls the trigger.

> Vito [Genovese] told me that when [Gaetano] Reina saw him he started to smile and wave his hand. When he done that, Vito blew his head off with a shotgun.
> —"Lucky" Luciano

There are times when a friend doesn't intend to hurt you but his selfishness, stupidity, or negligence brings you down.

In an earlier chapter, I spoke of wiseguy John Petrucelli, who was murdered for not only hiding his friend Gus Farace, but also refusing to kill Farace when the boss found out. Farace knew he broke Mob rules and therefore knew he was putting Petrucelli's life in danger when he asked his friend for help. No matter how you look at it, Petrucelli died for Farace, who obviously cared little about him.

In the pen, I knew a Boston wiseguy who was serving a life sentence for multiple murders. The wiseguy had some "friends" on the street who remained loyal to him. One day, while I was waiting to use the phone after him, he began to speak loosely with whoever was on the other end of the line. He talked about collecting loan shark debts and other rackets he was still running from the can.

When he hung up the phone, a Jersey wiseguy who had also overheard his conversation while waiting for another phone said to him, "You should watch what you say, the phones are tapped."

The Boston wiseguy replied, "I don't give a fuck, I'm already serving life."

"But your friend isn't," replied the Jersey wiser-guy.

The Boston wiseguy looked like a deer caught in headlights. He was exposed for what he was: a guy who didn't care much about his so-called friends.

> God deliver us from our friends. We can handle the enemy.
>
> —General George S. Patton

How many times in your life has a friend asked you to do something you didn't want to do, but you felt like you couldn't say no? It's usually that "friend" who brings you down.

I don't discourage you from standing by a friend in need; that's what life is about. But a true friend will never intentionally endanger you. If so, it's time to question that friendship.

Sometimes, you must say no. It's strictly business.

LESSON 61

The Mafia Spends Very Little on Office Supplies*:
Cutting Overhead

I was shaking down this guy, Larry, who owned a large auto parts distributorship. Larry made tons of bread and had no problem throwing a few crumbs my way. Then one day, the payments stopped. Larry claimed his business no longer made a profit.

I was standing in Larry's office when he cried poverty. He was wearing python-skin shoes, kicked up onto a Louis Whatever-the-King desk. He had a thirty-thousand-dollar Bulgari watch on his wrist, a fifty-dollar cigar was stinking up his office, and a giant TV hung on the wall. Outside his office, at least fifty people worked at their desks.

"Bullshit!" I told him. "I want my fuckin' money."

"I'll show you my books." Larry reached into a file cabinet.

"I'm in a rush," I said. "Have 'em ready tomorrow. I'll be back."

I wasn't in a rush, but the fact was I wouldn't have known his ass from his spreadsheet.

The next day, I returned with an accountant, figuring Larry had cooked the books and that the accountant could prove it. I left the accountant in Larry's office and told him to call me when he was done.

I was so sure I was being jerked around that I set aside an hour that night just to kick Larry's ass.

My accountant called me a few hours later and said, "This guy's legit."

"How can that be?" I was amazed.

"He's playing Mr. Big Shot. He's got a ten-thousand-square-foot

---

*Woody Allen, *Getting Even*.

warehouse when he only needs five. Ten good salespeople can handle his accounts; he's got fifty. He's got four fancy cars leased through the business, one of which is yours."

I was silent. Although I wanted Larry to fix his business, I wasn't willing to give up my car.

"Louie, he blows money left and right. He could run his operation out of a two-car garage and cut his overhead in half."

"Anything else?" I asked.

"Yeah, his employees are stealing toilet paper."

I paid the accountant and gave Larry three months to put his shop in order. He did, and my money started rolling in again.

Scrutinize your expenses. Every nickel you cut from overhead is an extra nickel in your purse.

By the way, as I mentioned, I didn't give up my leased car. Shortly after, I was in a bad automobile accident. Extra lesson: you always get what you deserve, and with irony.

LESSON 62

Social Clubs Have Solid Steel Doors—That Are Always Open: An Open-Door Policy

EVER see an Italian-American soccer club with a dozen hefties loitering outside? Either the team's alumni really let themselves go, or it's a Mafia social club.

Every mobster has one primary hangout where he holds court. Sometimes, the boss is standing out front or taking a walk-talk around the block with a criminal associate. But he's usually inside playing cards.

Although most clubs have solid steel doors with a peephole, they're totally accessible to members of the organization. It's a place where every "employee" can visit the boss to discuss business.

> He plays politics every day and night in the year, and his headquarters bears the inscription, "Never Closed."
> —William L. Riordan, *Plunkitt of Tammany Hall*

If the boss is always so available, you might wonder how he gets anything accomplished.

To start with, the boss weeds out people who waste his time. Wiseguys who come to him with every shit problem lose the privilege of visiting him any time they wish. They're weeded out by those unathletic guys in front of the soccer club; in your case, a secretary. But any person who isn't on your list of nuisances should be granted access to your office.

A boss who closes his door to his employees ties his own hands. When someone controls the information that reaches you, that person controls you. Allowing, for example, only three people into your office is equal to placing yourself in the custody of those three people—something you should never do.

An open-door policy gives you an open view of the office. Every last fart will find your ears, and that's the best way to keep a handle on your employees at all times.

LESSON 63

Don't Bother Me Now!: The Value of Interruptions

.

ONCE your door is open, you'll be exposed to plenty of interruptions.

As I said in the last chapter, you've got to weed out those regular nuisances, but aside from them, welcome all other interruptions. I learned something in a dark place that shined new light on interruptions.

In prison, I lent advice to literally hundreds of men who came to me with every kind of problem you can imagine: what should I tell my wife; how should I handle my son; should I kill my lawyer . . .

After a while, the interruptions got to me.

In certain prisons, the cells have heavy steel doors. At the center of each door is a rectangular window with reinforced glass. When cons need privacy, they tuck a piece of cardboard into the frame around the glass. This standard practice prevents other cons from gazing in while you're on the can or jerking off. When you're done, the cardboard is removed.

I began to put that piece of cardboard on my glass and leave it there all day: Do Not Disturb! I was finally alone with my thoughts, and had chunks of uninterrupted time to read and write.

One day, an Israeli gangster approached me on the tier as I was returning to my cell from chow. Just before I hung the cardboard up, he said to me, "You shouldn't block people out. You've helped a lot of guys in here."

"They can be pains in the asses," I said.

"What if someone is thinking about suicide and needs to talk to you?"

I've known men who have killed themselves in prison, so that caught my attention. The next day, I left my door wide open. Not only did I lend an ear and offer advice to men in need, but I benefited from the interruptions as well.

Here's how: If I was in the middle of writing something when a con poked his head in, I'd put my pen down to talk with him. When he left, I'd return to my paper and find that my mind was filled with fresh ideas. If I was struggling with a problem when interrupted, I found, after speaking to someone, that I'd return to that problem with a solution in mind. What happened?

My brain, given an opportunity to roam at will while I bullshitted with Bubba, C-Train, or Tex, continued to work subconsciously on the problem. A brief distraction is similar to sleeping on a problem and waking up with an answer. I realized that interruptions are a part of our perfect world.

I received another benefit from welcoming interruptions: the more glimpses I had into different personalities, the better I understood human nature. And the more we understand human nature, the greater our chances for success.

Most important, I helped a lot of people. So can you.

LESSON 64

The Bail Money's in the Bedside Drawer:
Get It Right Ahead of Time

WHAT'S the worst that can happen? A chemical spill? A sexual harassment suit? A rotten news story? *E. coli* in the cafeteria?

No one anticipates problems better than the Mob.

Like most mobsters, I thought I'd never go to jail. I thought I was too smart to get caught. And yet, like most mobsters, I was ready, just in case.

I made sure everyone around me knew exactly what to do if I was pinched.

My cousin Don was to get bail money together and hire an attorney. Franky Stitches was to gather the titles to my cars, all under different people's names, and sell the vehicles before they were confiscated. Johnny on the Avenue was to hold my jewelry in a safe deposit box. Benny was to take over my loan shark book and continue collections, while Juney would assume leadership of my crew and collect debts from fences for hijacked loads. Ally the Whisper would look out for my family. Last, I asked a friend on the fringe to report weekly to me on prison visits so I could keep a handle on operations and make decisions if necessary.

If you see a need to make contingency plans similar to these mentioned above, you're knee-deep in shit and I feel for you. For all others, use this extreme example as a guide to prepare for worst-case scenarios you're sure to encounter.

Wiseguys lead daring lives. Aware of how unpredictable fate can be, most mobsters get it right, *ahead* of time.

LESSON 65

Don't Build Yankee Stadium, Just Supply the Concrete: Spotting New Rackets

YESTERDAY'S Mafia wore pin-striped suits and fedoras. Today's Mafia can be seen wearing T-shirts and Levi's.

Considering the original business approach of Levi Strauss, the founder of Levi Strauss & Co., his blue jeans are entirely appropriate for modern mobsters, and an apt metaphor for the Mafia's methods.

Strauss was an immigrant who landed in America just before the Gold Rush. In 1848, gold was found in California, and by the following year every dreamer in the world had trekked west. They shot for the stars and scraped their fingers to the bone digging for that one shiny nugget that would allow them a life of luxury. Few found gold. Most became disenchanted and returned home. Some wandered aimlessly, gambling and whoring their lives away, ending up as worn down as the earth they blasted apart.

Unlike those dreamers, Strauss could spot the real nugget. Wagonloads of men were landing in California every day. They needed the basics to live and work: food, clothing, shovels, picks, pans, boots, buckets, combs, and handkerchiefs. Strauss opened a general store in San Francisco—Gold Rush Central—and sold every item the workers needed to panhandle, including his own twist on work pants: denim blue jeans.

Strauss never sought the glitter of gold, but became one of the wealthiest men the Rush ever produced. The blue jeans he manufactured are still worn by all of us today, including mobsters.

Smart mobsters operate using the same business principle as Strauss did. They may not get the big contract to build Yankee Stadium, but they set themselves up to supply a million ancillary needs.

A perceptive mobster can analyze any large project in terms of the moneymaking potential it represents.

Let's look at Yankee Stadium. To build something that big, an enormous amount of debris must be hauled away from the site, some of it getting recycled. The contract for cement might be worth twenty million. Then there's steel, rebar, wiring, plumbing, and carpentry. And how about food for thousands of workers?

Think about that stadium for a few minutes and let your mind open up to the profit possibilities. Sod. Dirt. Plastic seats. Electronic signboards. Flagpoles. The list is getting long and we're just getting started. And construction can take years.

> Activities of the criminal underworld are, by their nature, kaleidoscopic, constantly responding to shifts in market conditions and exploiting the myriad money-making opportunities provided by the legitimate world.
> —Paul Lunde, *Organized Crime*

Chicago mobster Murray "The Camel" Humphreys was always looking for the next cash cow. He found it, quite literally, in 1930. While every mobster was warring over bootleg whiskey, Humphreys noticed that milk was in greater demand than booze, and set up Meadowmoor Dairies to meet the demand. By the way, you can thank Meadowmoor for introducing the "sell by" date on milk containers; kids getting sick from spoiled milk was bad publicity the Mob didn't need.

Like Levi Strauss, the Mafia can spot gold that doesn't glitter, even when it's squirting from a cow's sack.

Today, the Mafia operates worldwide in more than forty countries. But stay legit. Strauss sells blue jeans in over sixty countries; he outdid the Mob three to two.

LESSON 66

Give the IRS Their Vig:
What We've Learned from Al Capone

ONLY taxmen will hunt you down with more persistence than the Mob. When the law was unable to put the cuffs on Al Capone, they turned to the IRS. Trying to build a tax evasion case, the IRS combed through Capone's tax returns and drove around Chicago visiting stores where Capone shopped. They added up the cost of Capone's rugs and furniture, anything they could prove he owned.

When the IRS nailed him, Capone offered to pay what he owed. It was too late; the IRS sent him to prison.

After Capone went down, word spread around the Mob: give Uncle Sam his vig.

When a businessman owns a tangible business and owes the Mob money, the Mob will sometimes force the businessman to do a "bust out," in which they clean out his inventory, collect any debts owed to his business while letting his bills pile up, and then torch his joint and make him fork over the insurance check.

> Senator Tobey: "You must have in your mind something you've done that you can speak of to your credit as an American citizen. If so, what is it?"
> Frank Costello: "I paid my tax."
> —Kefauver Committee investigating organized crime,
> 1951

The IRS doesn't refer to their collection procedures as a "bust out," but they can be just as ruthless. They'll confiscate everything you own until you're even.

The Mob may kill you, but the IRS will torture you without

letting you die. Even smart mobsters who are experts at beating the system don't mess with Uncle Sam.

Black gangster Leroy "Nicky" Barnes ruled Harlem with an iron fist but was terrified of Uncle Sam. He filed taxes every year on a quarter of a million dollars in "miscellaneous income," to keep the IRS off his back. The law eventually nailed Barnes, but it wasn't the taxman who did it.

A large percentage of Americans fudge a little on their taxes. The bigger you get, the more enemies you attract, and the more careful you'd better be! Give Uncle Sam his vig.

LESSON 67

Victory Without Follow-up Is Like Pasta Without Dessert:
Crisis Management

MARCH 21, 1980. Ten o'clock at night on a Philly street. A maroon Chevy is parked in front of a row of attached houses. Don Angelo Bruno sits in the car's passenger seat after being driven home by a member of his crime family. As the two chat in the parked car, a third man approaches and puts the barrel of a shotgun to Bruno's head. There is the subtle click of a trigger, followed by a loud blast. And the brain that ruled Philly for twenty years is blown out of its shell. The longtime don of the Philadelphia Mob has been forced into retirement.

The Philadelphia crime family was in major crisis.

The culprit behind the hit, Anthony "Tony Bananas" Caponigro, was the family consigliere. A consigliere is a position that normally requires wisdom; Caponigro's mind would prove to be as bent as a banana.

At the time, no one in the family knew who was behind the hit. As consigliere, Caponigro was sought out for advice. But instead of addressing the troops with a commanding air, or appointing a PR man to ease the tension, Caponigro hid out in Jersey waiting to hear what developed. He had no strategy; he just assumed that everyone would find out he killed Bruno somehow, and fall in line behind him out of fear. He exhibited no diplomacy, and saw no reason to placate Bruno's pals, who were naturally angered by his death.

When Caponigro's own men asked him what their next move was, he told them, "Don't worry about nothin'." Then he partied up a storm, celebrating his "victory."

MOB RULES

Wishful thinking is not a substitute for a legitimate crisis communication strategy.
—Steve Adubato, *What Were They Thinking?: Crisis Communication*

Caponigro was under quite a delusion. Less than a month after Bruno's hit, Caponigro's nude body was found in the trunk of a car. He'd been beaten, strangled, stabbed, and shot. A few hundred dollars in cash had been stuffed down his throat, and up his ass.

Caponigro's first mistake was killing Bruno, the "Gentle Don," who was well liked by most of the family and had a strong relationship with the other families. With a little propaganda, however, Caponigro might have lowered people's high opinion of Bruno and made a case for his actions. Caponigro's second, more perilous mistake was believing that a major crisis would sort itself out.

Because of Caponigro's utter failure to acknowledge or deal with the crisis that followed Bruno's murder, civil war broke out within the Philadelphia crime family. Twenty-eight wiseguys were stabbed, shot, and blown to bits before a temporary truce halted the violence. A short while later, hostilities began again.

Tony Bananas was bananas.

DECEMBER 16, 1985. Evening rush hour in midtown Manhattan. Christmas shoppers swarm the streets. A black Lincoln pulls to the curb in front of a steakhouse. Just as two well-dressed men get out of the car, four assassins wearing white trench coats and Russian fur hats approach, firing a hail of bullets. The most powerful Mafia boss and underboss in the country lie dead in pools of blood. The assassins disappear into the crowd.

The Gambino crime family was in major crisis.

Any brute can shoot people on the street, but in the hours that followed, John Gotti, the culprit behind the double hit of Paul Castellano and Tommy Bilotti, proved himself to be a master of crisis management.

> Perseus fell upon all his enemies before they knew or even suspected and seized by violence the throne he had won by crime.
>
> —Livy, *A History of Rome*

In all probability, the hit should have resulted in an all-out war within the Gambino family, or a bloody war against the other New York families. The following is how further bloodshed was avoided.

The Gambino family demanded to know who was behind the hit, as did the other New York families. The Mafia doesn't like publicity, and every major news source in the country was covering the hit.

Gotti wasn't sure he'd be readily accepted by his own family as their new don. Therefore, he recruited a PR person everyone liked: weak, aging, but respected mobster Joe Gallo (no relation to "Crazy Joe" Gallo). Gallo immediately called a meeting with the family capos and assured them that the family was intact. Gotti then sent messages to the other families saying that the Gambinos were investigating the hit themselves, and didn't need outside help.

Following the hit on Pope John Paul I in 1978, Vatican officials, suspected of culpability, played the same game as Gotti, telling the Italian government they were investigating the pope's death themselves, and didn't need outside help. Whether American mobsters or Roman Curia, Italians trace their philosophy to Machiavelli.

With the other families on the sidelines awaiting news, Gotti had a small time frame in which to consolidate power within his own family. He had his PR man, Gallo, call a second meeting with the capos. This time, Gallo proposed a vote for the next boss. Gotti was no student of political science, but instinctively relied on an old politburo trick in which everyone mimicked Stalin's vote—or else. By then, the capos realized who the real culprit was and voted unanimously in favor of Gotti—or else.

A good step forward, but this was no time to rest—this wasn't a Boy Scout troop voting on a new leader. These were killers who could still plan a counterstroke.

Next, Gotti turned potential enemies into friends. By taking over the family, Gotti had moved the center of power from Staten Island and Brooklyn to Queens. To appease bloodthirsty Brooklynites who felt slighted, Gotti appointed charismatic Brooklyn capo Frankie DeCicco as his official underboss. To appease old-timers who viewed Gotti as a young upstart, he appointed elderly and senile mobster Joe Piney as consigliere.

Gotti also promoted tough wiseguys from key neighborhoods knowing that, in return for high positions, they'd owe him their loyalty.

Without another drop of blood spilled and before the week was up, members of the Gambino family lined up outside Gotti's Manhattan headquarters to kiss their new don. The other families, though vexed by Gotti's actions, were at least satisfied that the Gambino household was in order, and permitted Gotti to carry on as boss.

At this very same juncture during Caponigro's coup, fellow mobsters were inserting bills into his ass like a vending machine.

In the event of a crisis, act fast, appoint PR people to get the right message across, and use aggressive diplomacy. Whether dealing with employees or the public, trade favors to win support. A crisis does not solve itself.

LESSON 68

The Power of an Elite Circle:
Why the Mob Opens and Closes the Books

THE Mafia is composed of select men who have mastered the streets and proven their earning ability. Entry into this elite circle is difficult during ordinary times and impossible when the "books" are closed. Although gaining entry has become a little easier today, in years past street guys paid their dues for decades.

Even if it's an illusion with more headaches than it's worth, a group with restricted membership offers people a sense of status. The harder it is to get into an elite circle, the harder people will try.

Yacht clubs and country clubs work on the same premise as the Mob: money and connections are required for entry. And everyone is dying to get in. Or, in the Mob's case, killing to get in.

Rao's is the hardest restaurant to get into in Manhattan. The food is no better than any other top Italian restaurant in the city, but Rao's waiting list is much longer.

> A table at Rao's? Forgetaboutit.
>
> —*The New York Times*

Why? Rao's has made a habit of denying people entry. And they really don't give a shit who you are. In fact, the more important you are, the more they enjoy saying no.

Part owner Frank "Frankie No" Pellegrino got his nickname from turning people away. All customers, including celebrities, wait weeks, sometimes months, for a reservation. Rao's is a small restaurant, with only ten tables. By allowing in a limited clientele, Rao's has translated the concept of an elite circle into the restaurant business—and everyone is dying to get in, even mobsters, plenty of whom are also turned away.

MOB RULES

Chicago boss Anthony Accardo was married to a woman named Clarice. Accardo's daily life rubbed off on Clarice and she decided to start her own elite circle, "The Vodka Club."

The Vodka Club was a select group of women, all wives of high-ranking mobsters. The group got together and played cards, gossiped, and, as the name suggests, drank. Members paid monthly dues and used the kitty to pay for vacations. The wife of every hoodlum in Chicago wanted to be a member. I can only wonder how many Mafia wives pushed their husbands to commit bigger crimes and rise in the family, only to gain entrance for them into the Vodka Club.

In business, a boss can create a "top sellers circle" or the like. Every good salesman will give that extra push to get in, and stay in.

You can get creative when establishing an elite circle and turn a gimmick into big profits. Just keep it on the up-and-up, and make sure it serves a genuine purpose.

LESSON 69

Give the Spic Bastard a Call!: Hiring the Best Person,
Regardless of Race, Creed, or Sexual Orientation

IN 1924, a hijacker named Joe Howard made an anti-Semitic remark to a Jewish thug named Jake Guzik. Al Capone heard about the remark and shot Howard six times in front of witnesses.

A few years before Capone defended Guzik over that ethnic slur, he married an Irish girl named Mae Coughlin. Mixed matches were uncommon back then. Italians usually married their own. In fact, Capone began a liberal tradition in the Chicago Mob that allowed Jews, Greeks, blacks, even a Welshman into the Outfit, and they all turned out to be big earners.

> We got Jews, we got Polacks, we got Greeks, we got all kinds.
>
> —Chicago mobster Jackie Cerone

In the 1930s, while the American South was denying blacks equal rights, future Louisiana Mob boss Carlos Marcello named his first pub The Brown Bomber, after the African-American boxing champion Joe Louis.

While Capone was welcoming non-Italians into Chicago's underworld and Marcello was glorifying a black fighter in bigot country, the New York Mafia was struggling with the question of allowing other ethnicities into the fold. The hard-liners, led by Salvatore Maranzano, distrusted non-Italians and banned business relations with outsiders. The progressives, led by "Lucky" Luciano, insisted that racial and religious prejudice was sheer ignorance that would deny the Mafia scores of talented men.

The dispute was resolved in Manhattan on September 10, 1931, when Maranzano was murdered by Luciano's hit men.

To literally add insult to injury, Luciano dispatched four Jewish assassins to dispose of Maranzano. From that day on, the New York Mafia families would require Italian blood for official membership—Luciano always compromised—but would open their doors to anyone who could earn a buck.

To this day, just about every New York Mafia crew has a trusted Jew in its ranks. There were two tough Jews on my own indictment, listed as members of my crew.

> I think [mobsters are] the most unracist people in the world. They're just greedy. The only color they care about is green, the color of money. They don't give a shit about any nationality, any religion, any anything.
>
> —Sammy "The Bull" Gravano

Mobsters are loose with racial slurs and love ethnic jokes, but they make money with Irish, black, Greek, Russian, and Chinese mobsters. Not because society compels them to do so—they obviously don't fret too much over society's mores—but because it's the smart thing to do.

As for women, the American Mafia will do business with them, but considers them second-class citizens. The Italian Mafia has developed a more liberal attitude toward women.

In Italy, Anna Mazza, nicknamed "The Black Widow," controlled her own crime family after her husband was murdered in 1976. She cultivated relationships with politicians and guided the family's economic interests.

Pupetta Maresca, or "Madame Camorra," personally gunned down her husband's murderer in broad daylight. After a stint in prison, she returned to the streets with an honorable reputation and took over many rackets normally controlled by men.

Maria Serraino was a female "don" sentenced to life in prison, and Giusy Vitale, referred to as "the godmother," headed one of Sicily's most powerful crime families.

> The women became clan managers, entrepreneurs, and bodyguards. They were better at business, less obsessed with ostentatious shows of power, and less eager for conflict.
>
> —Roberto Saviano, *Gomorrah*

Immacolata Capone, who secured building contracts from local politicians, was the driving force behind the Mob's climb to the top of the construction industry in Naples.

Although she was protected by female bodyguards, most of her soldiers were men. As further proof of the Italian Mafia's equal treatment of women, hit men gunned her down on the street when, as a boss, she overstepped her boundaries. Now that's equal rights, coming and going.

In the seventies, Yugoslav dictator Marshal Tito received a visit from future British prime minister Margaret Thatcher. While discussing Madame Mao, who seemed to be interfering with politics in China following her husband's death, Tito seized an opportunity to take a jab at Thatcher.

"I don't believe in women interfering in politics," Tito said.

Thatcher, sharp as a razor, responded, "I don't interfere with politics. I am politics."

LESSON 70

A Little Give and Take: Hospitality

SICILIAN Mafia boss Benedetto Spera was on the lam for years. While in hiding, Spera needed the help of countless hoodlums, some of whom took him into their households. Since harboring a fugitive is illegal, all the families who helped Spera risked their freedom.

To avoid capture, Spera's loyal underlings shuffled him around in the dead of night, carried him up and down mountains, and splashed through mud and donkey shit.

As a guest in his men's houses, Spera kicked his feet up on the sofa and threw around his weight. As if bossing his men around in front of their families wasn't enough humiliation, he ran their wives into the ground with incessant requests.

> His character and manners made his power hateful.
> —Plutarch, *The Life of Theseus*

Spera's men were caught on tape complaining about his abuse: "I've barely been home. I'm the real fugitive," "We've been his slaves."

Not surprisingly, Spera was dimed. Whoever made the call must have hung up the phone and danced a jig. Imagine the party Spera's men had when he was led away in cuffs. The police probably thought they were being shot at while it was just the sound of champagne corks popping.

In contrast to Spera, another Sicilian Mafia boss, Bernardo Provenzano, was on the lam for forty years. Nobody gave him up. Provenzano enjoyed the hospitality of countless households and showed his appreciation any way he could. After his hosts served him dinner, Provenzano washed dishes and swept the floors.

When Provenzano was finally captured, he asked the arresting officer if a snitch had given him up. He must have been relieved to learn that it was sheer investigative work that did him in.

Provenzano's gratitude toward the many people who fed, clothed, and hid him for four decades was appreciated, and no one had betrayed him.

When you're the boss, people will fall over themselves to be hospitable toward you. Don't take it for granted, like Spera did. Appreciate it like Provenzano. And of course, always be hospitable to your own guests.

LESSON 71

Tip the Coat Check: Charity

MY friend "Fat George" DiBello was the caretaker for John Gotti's social club in Queens. While tending bar on a busy night, George scooped up a few hundred in tips. The majority of mobsters were generous, but one in particular stood out: Joe Watts.

> One thing Santo [Trafficante] did was tip. He tipped big-time.
>
> —Frank Ragano

If Joe asked George for a glass of water from the tap, he dropped a crisp hundred on the bar. When George refilled his glass, Joe left another hundred, and before Joe left the club, he'd drop a third. Three hundred bucks for two glasses of rusty tap water.

Joe Watts started out as a close confidant of Don Carlo Gambino. When Carlo died, Joe became a major earner and counselor to Paul Castellano. When Castellano was killed, Joe became the right-hand man of John Gotti. Few knights have survived the court intrigues of three different kings. Joe not only survived, but prospered under each king.

There's a long list of Darwinian traits responsible for Joe's survival, but being known as the most generous man in the Mob certainly helped.

I got close with Joe in the can. After I hired and fired several top-notch, jerk-off attorneys, Joe walked over to me and said, "Why not hire my lawyer?"

Joe called his lawyer, who then came to visit me in prison. After our visit, I decided to hire the lawyer and asked him the cost of his retainer.

"I'm already retained," he said. "Joe took care of it. He sent a guy to my office this morning."

It's common practice for a mobster to retain a lawyer to represent a potential witness against him; it's smart, not generous. But Joe owed me nothing. He and I weren't coconspirators or codefendants; Joe did this out of pure kindness and generosity.

> When a mobster died, Santo [Trafficante] would fly to that city, always with an envelope of money in hand for the widow.
>
> —Frank Ragano

Even in the Mob, charity is recognized as a virtue, and the Mob comes down hard on mobsters who use charities to defraud people.

In 1976, First Lady Rosalynn Carter attended a fund-raising event with cult leader Jim Jones. Jones later moved to Guyana and orchestrated the slaughter of nine hundred men, women, and children.

Gambino soldier Jimmy Eppolito must have heard about the First Lady's naïveté. He decided to take her for a ride, recruiting the first lady to promote his charity, the International Children's Appeal.

Eppolito was skimming millions of dollars from the charity. I guess he felt he deserved the money more than poor, destitute children with swollen bellies and flies landing on their eyelids. He also used the fund to launder money from his drug operations. Nice guy.

Mrs. Carter was fooled and invited Eppolito to Washington so she could take some photos with him. Mrs. Carter with a Mafia hit man. Mrs. Carter with a savage cult leader. If we're still curious as to the identity of Jack the Ripper, it's worth flipping through the pages of Mrs. Carter's old photo albums.

Anyway, the media had a field day with her Mafia photos. Comedians, late-night talk show hosts, everyone got in on the joke.

But the Mafia wasn't laughing. A contract immediately went out on Eppolito and he was whacked. The Mafia was disgraced by his fraudulence because they take great pride in acting straight up when it comes to charities.

In 2004, Queens borough president Helen Marshall honored reputed Genovese mobster Anthony "Tough Tony" Federici for his service to the community. In 2007, New York state senator Serphin Maltese honored reputed Bonanno soldier Vito Grimaldi for his community service.

> [Capone] says we all got to tighten our belts a little to help those poor guys who haven't got any jobs.
>
> —Capone henchman

The giving goes all the way back to the early days of the Mob. Frank Costello chaired many fund-raisers, including the men's division of the Salvation Army. Black gangster Bumpy Johnson gave out turkeys for Thanksgiving in his poor Harlem neighborhood. Louisiana boss Carlos Marcello once gave ten grand to the Girl Scouts of America. That's a lot of cookies. He asked them to keep it quiet. They didn't—they squealed. Remember that sign above Marcello's door, "THREE CAN KEEP A SECRET IF TWO ARE DEAD"? I'm fairly sure he knew that news of his donation would leak, but I guess he figured it would be good for his image.

Mobsters, like businessmen, know that it's smart to give, especially when a little press comes with it. It's cheap advertising. But mobsters also give when nobody is looking.

I never met a mobster, myself included, who didn't hand a twenty to a panhandler or windshield washer, those guys who used to run up to your car and descend upon your windshield with a squeegee in Manhattan. Maybe the tip made us feel better for all the bad we'd done, or maybe we hoped it offered us protection from evil, like garlic.

Instead of just begging for change, the windshield washers were offering a service. Unlike me and my friends, they were willing to work and not steal. Sadly, most New Yorkers didn't agree with this rationale and were annoyed by their presence. In the 1990s, Mayor

Rudolph Giuliani, responding to public outcry, passed a law to sweep squeegee men off the streets. With no skills, opportunities, or assistance, many windshield washers turned to petty crime, robbing the public who wouldn't allow them to offer a service in return for a coin.

In seventeenth-century England, begging was considered a public nuisance, and beggars were removed from the streets. What followed in that same century were the Great Plague and the Great Fire of London, which wiped out 80 percent of the city.

New York was hit hard by 9/11. I'm not saying that God punished us for the squeegee men; to think so would be insane. But when tragedy strikes, it's nice to have a clear conscience.

While John Gotti, Jr., may have committed all the crimes the government has accused him of, there was a charitable side to him as well. In 1912, the U.S. Postmaster General instituted a "Letters to Santa" program, in which needy children write letters to Santa, addressed to the North Pole. The children usually praise their own good behavior and ask Santa to reward them with a Christmas gift. Ordinarily, businesspeople "adopt" a letter and fulfill a child's wish.

John Gotti, Jr., would acquire a stack of letters addressed to the North Pole, then hand them to Fat George along with a few grand in cash. Fat George would drive to Toys "R" Us, fulfill the children's specific wishes, load the presents into his van, and deliver them.

> Many a poor family in Chicago thinks I'm Santa Claus.
> —Al Capone

When I heard the news that Junior had been acquitted in court for the fourth time, I recalled his dedication to needy children and wondered if his anonymous generosity had protected him in his own time of need.

Have compassion for the have-nots. Giving comes back around tenfold, and protects us from evil, like garlic.

LESSON 72

Eat, Drink, and Be Productive:
The Only Bribe I'll Advise You to Make

THIS guy, Tony, lost his job and started a card game in Ozone Park. It was Mob territory, so Tony asked a local wiseguy for a license to operate. He was open about a month when I bumped into him and asked how his game was going.

"Makin' money?"

"Shit," he said, disgusted. "I'm gonna close down if it don't pick up."

"I ain't lookin' to shake you down," I assured him. "You're already wit' somebody."

"No, I ain't lyin'. Maybe it's the spot."

Tony's game was located in the back room of a storage warehouse and the players had to walk around pallets of merchandise to get there, but gamblers will trek into the Amazon rain forest and wrestle anacondas to play cards.

"It's not the spot," I said. "You serve food?"

"Peanuts. I put out a few bowls."

"What are they, elephants? Put out Sternos wit' ziti an' manicotti. What can it cost you, a hundred bucks a night? An' serve liquor to keep them loose. A few drinks an' they're happy to lose their pants."

"You think my problem is food?"

"Sure, everybody loves to eat."

A free meal is never free, but nobody knows that. As a mobster, I'd blow ten grand in Atlantic City and brag that they gave me a prime rib dinner on comp. Big fucking deal. A measly steak. I could have purchased a herd of bulls for ten grand.

Tony took my advice and started to serve food at his card game. Word spread and his joint filled up. I bumped into him a few months later.

> After business, Carlos [Marcello] would provide his faithful with food and drink.
>
> —John H. Davis, *Mafia Kingfish*

"I'm doin' great," he told me. "The food thing worked. A few moochers show up to eat, but even they play long enough to cover their meals."

"Cops or firemen?"

"Both. How'd you know?"

"They think they got somethin' comin'," I replied. "They're worse than us."

My cousin Don is a partner in an auto body shop that has fifty employees. Every Friday afternoon, he orders twenty pizza pies with toppings. His workers dance the salsa, a slice in one hand, a wrench in the other.

A lot of companies feed their employees to keep them at their desks and get them back to work faster. It's a sensible management practice, and one that dates back to at least the Renaissance.

During the Renaissance, Brunelleschi was an Italian architect who also did a little jail time. When Brunelleschi was building his famous dome in Florence, he fed his workers "aloft in order to foil idlers." He also did not want them to waste time walking up and down three hundred steps and return to work exhausted.

Lunch meetings, dinner dates, birthdays, and banquets; everything we do revolves around food. Look at all the chef shows. Ever think how much of this world is shaped in a restaurant? Next time you're there, look around at the tables. A man is proposing, friendships are beginning, families are laughing, businessmen are conniving, mobsters are whispering. Everyone's bullshitting with a forkful of food in their mouths.

> [Tony] Bananas always hosted a major Mob dinner on Thursdays. Guys would come from Philly, Atlantic City,

and New York for an evening of good Italian food and
drink, and sometimes we fed forty or fifty guys.
—George Fresolone and Robert J. Wagman,
Blood Oath

Although the source varies, the story comes down to us that Queen Marie Antoinette was told that the people of France were starving.

"They're poor, and can't afford bread," said a concerned member of her court.

"Let them eat cake," she responded.

We may laugh at her naïveté, but she was right. The problem was that she never really baked the friggin' cakes and handed them out to her subjects. Had she, it might've saved her ass—or head.

The United States represents 5 percent of the world's population and locks up 25 percent of the world's prisoners. How do we keep so many prisoners from rioting? In part, we give them cake. I'm not kidding. In prison, I've seen thousands of men receive sentences in which the punishment far outweighed the crime. They complained but never talked of revolt.

Then one evening, chow was served without dessert; the kitchen ran out of sweets. In less than a minute, trays were flying and tables were overturned.

The unit manager, a civilian administrator who ranks above the prison guards, called me into his office, knowing I had a good rapport with my fellow prisoners. He asked me if I could calm them until he was able to send out for ice cream pops.

An hour later, I was amazed to see a chow hall full of hardened cons as happy as babies sucking on pacifiers.

Sigmund Freud saw human behavior as driven by what he called "life instincts." Our strongest instinct, he said, is to seek food. Help people find it and you're the boss.

At least once a week, every classy mobster puts out a big spread at his social club. He's buying loyalty with food. Often, the way to people's hearts is through their stomachs.

LESSON 73

I'm Comin' on the Heist Tonight: The Hands-on Boss

IN the early nineties, the second civil war in thirty years broke out in New York's Colombo family. The Persico faction was warring with the Orena faction over who would be the family's undisputed boss.

Carmine "The Snake" Persico was leader of the Persico faction. He had previously established himself on the Brooklyn battlefield and had the scars to prove it. Persico was shot in the face, qualifying him for a Purple Heart—except the Mafia doesn't award medals.

Victor "Little Vic" Orena was the leader of the rebel faction; mostly Young Turks and a few old-timers.

Persico had always been a hands-on boss, but he was incarcerated during the second war, sort of like being a POW. His men fought on without him.

Orena, a free man during the war, was also a hands-on boss. He was well liked by his men, extremely accessible, and always willing to get dirty.

While the war was being fought, Orena could have hopped a flight to Bermuda and commanded his forces from a beachfront resort. After all, Persico wasn't on the battlefield. But everyone knew, including Orena, that Persico would've been in the fray if he could have been.

To compete with a man who had a hands-on reputation like Persico, Orena had to be a battlefield commander. This wasn't hard for Orena. I knew Little Vic, and it wasn't in his nature to yell orders from an ivory tower. If Orena was spotted in a tower, it was because he was helping his men pour boiling oil on the heads of invading troops.

Orena was a hands-on boss who went on missions and slept on floors alongside his men when they went to the mattresses.

It was a long, hard-fought war claiming many lives. The Persico faction won by default when Orena was captured by the FBI and sent to prison for life. But it could have gone either way, because soldiers are willing to lay down their lives for a hands-on boss.

Likewise, employees are willing to work harder and longer hours for a hands-on boss.

Get out there. Meet the people. Visit the stores, the warehouse, the shipping room, and the assembly lines. Shake hands with the cashiers and truck drivers. Put on a pair of Levi's and get dirty.

If you plan to compete with companies that have hands-on bosses, you'd better be one yourself.

Like Persico and Orena, archrivals Napoleon Bonaparte and the Duke of Wellington were hands-on bosses.

Wellington credited the little Corsican by saying, "[Napoleon's] presence on the battlefield was worth 40,000 men."

Knowing he was confronting an attendant leader such as Napoleon, Wellington also had to be hands-on.

In being so, he ultimately defeated Napoleon and once remarked about his own success, "The real reason why I succeeded in my own campaigns is because I was always on the spot—I saw everything, and did everything for myself."

LESSON 74

A Tough Guy Has Balls. A Smart Guy
Has Crystal Balls: Foresight

WHILE the early Sicilian Americans, like Maranzano, were closing the doors to outsiders, "Lucky" Luciano had the foresight to see that America was a melting pot and that maximum potential in the rackets would depend on harmonious relationships with other ethnic gangs. As noted earlier, Luciano's compromise—and every great leader must compromise—was that only full-blooded Italians could be initiated into the *borgatas*, or crime families. But each *borgata* was allowed, even encouraged, to work with non-Italians.

Because of Luciano's foresight, the Mafia drew scores of talented men who carried them through a prosperous century.

Meyer Lansky and Bugsy Siegel, two Jews credited with the vision of Las Vegas, were friends with Luciano.

While the New York and Chicago godfathers recognized Vegas's massive profit potential and sent henchmen to infiltrate the casinos, Florida boss Santo Trafficante missed the bus. Trafficante thought Havana, Cuba, would be the next gambling hot spot, and dumped his men and money into Cuba's Riviera Hotel and Casino. It was a fairly safe investment since Trafficante had the dictator of Cuba, Fulgencio Batista, in his pocket. Still, Trafficante hedged his bets, and supplied a young Cuban revolutionary, Fidel Castro, with money and guns just in case Castro seized control of the island, which he did. Trafficante's vision was dashed when Castro betrayed his Mafia supporters and shut the Mob out of Cuba. Trafficante was detained in a Cuban prison before being deported back to the States.

Trafficante was not about to lie down. First, he backed the counterrevolutionaries in the hopes of regaining his foothold in Cuba. Realizing this was a long shot, Trafficante made other plans. Here we see the importance of flexibility; if one dream is dashed, dream up another one.

The Castro revolution created a mass exodus of Cuban exiles. Nearly all the exiles landed in Miami. Trafficante, who spoke fluent Spanish, moved his Tampa-based operation to Miami, planting himself where he imagined the resulting economic boom would take place. In a short time, Trafficante established sole control over Miami's rackets while the rest of America's Mob bosses squabbled over pieces of Las Vegas.

> Joe had a genius for seeing something and knowing it would be worth something more later on.
> —Rose Kennedy, describing husband Joe Kennedy, a crooked businessman who made much of his fortune with gangsters

Trafficante never quit. He also envisioned an increasing number of northern retirees who would flee cold climates and seek the Florida sun to relieve their arthritic bones. What would old fogeys need? pondered Trafficante. Sunglasses? Bermuda shorts? Knee socks and sandals? Hearing aids? Geritol? Depends? We're getting warm—a hospital!

Trafficante invested in a hospital.

Around the same time, Trafficante's close friend and fellow Mafia don, Carlos Marcello, was in Louisiana buying tracts of cheap land in the path of the Dixie Freeway, hoping to reap windfall profits in federal highway funds.

Foresight. The best Mob bosses have it. To think ahead of the rest is to think among the best.

LESSON 75

Never Underestimate Your Opponent

RUSSIAN men are tough. Russian women are even tougher. Imagine how tough a Russian gangster is. I've known plenty of Russian gangsters, and it's no wonder to me that the Russians were the first to stop the Nazi war machine in its tracks.

The Russian-American Mob boss Marat Balagula was one of the toughest old men I've ever met. He was also a criminal genius. He partnered up with the Italian-American Mafia in zillion-dollar schemes. He also owned nightclubs and restaurants, even a diamond mine in Africa. (How does a Russian immigrant living in Brighton Beach come to own a diamond mine in Africa? Networking. Don't forget any lesson in this book.)

Balagula partnered with the Italians because they were organized and efficient, more so than his fellow Russians, who were busy establishing a tenuous foothold in Brooklyn, a place where the Italians had planted a flag over a century before Russian gangsters arrived. Partnering with Italians was a smart business move on Balagula's part, but his fellow Russian gangsters felt slighted and left out.

Vladimir Reznikov was one such Russian, who had set up a Russian-style Murder, Inc. He killed for himself and for others who were willing to pay for his services. A sadist, Reznikov tortured many of his victims. When Reznikov realized the scope of Balagula's rackets, he wanted in.

Reznikov introduced himself to Balagula by unloading a machine gun clip into Balagula's office, killing one of Balagula's friends. Having left his calling card, Reznikov followed up with a visit to one of Balagula's nightclubs. Here, he put a gun to Balagula's head and demanded a piece of every nickel Balagula earned.

At this point, a muffled explosion went off. It wasn't a gun, but a fart; Balagula shit his pants. He also suffered a massive heart attack, but he was up and around in no time. The fart aside, Balagula was not one to run, but would fight. He'd prove wilier than the sadistic punk he was up against.

Balagula wisely told Reznikov whatever he wanted to hear, then visited his business partners, the Italians, and told them what Reznikov did. He added that Reznikov was mouthing off around town, telling anyone who'd listen that the Italians had grown fat and weak, and therefore unable to protect their interests—in this case, Balagula.

Here's another excellent example of how history always repeats itself: On the eve of World War II, Japan had come to the same conclusion about the American people as Reznikov had about the Italian-American mobsters. Japanese leaders thought that Americans had grown fat and weak, unable to defend their interests.

Sure, a fair portion of America was, and still is, fat and weak. A diet of McDonald's, Dunkin' Donuts, and the like doesn't produce svelte athletic types.

But the young Marines dispatched to defend Guadalcanal and storm the beaches of Iwo Jima were lean, mean, fighting machines. The Japanese would eat their words; Reznikov was about to swallow the same meal.

When Reznikov returned to collect on his first installment from Balagula, a young man by the name of Joey Testa approached him, picking up speed as he walked. Joey wasn't fat; he was six feet tall, lean and muscular. Joey wasn't weak; some of the men he'd killed and hoisted into automobile trunks were three hundred pounds of literally dead weight. Joey didn't scream "*Semper fi,*" but like the valiant Marines who defended America's interests abroad, Joey believed in death before dishonor, and was eager to defend the Mafia's interests in Brooklyn.

Reznikov never saw it coming. He probably thought he was home free when Balagula stained his underwear. Balagula's insult was repaid in kind with bloodstains. Reznikov expired on a Brooklyn street, full of holes.

Never underestimate your opponent.

LESSON 76

Who Is Your Opponent?

IT'S usually apparent who your enemies are; as seen in the last chapter, you must never underestimate them. But what about those people who bide their time, exhibiting unique patience and hiding their ambitions? People you'd never consider opponents? They can be close friends, colleagues, even your number-one employee. How do you distinguish a loyal follower from an opportunist? And how do you neutralize that potential opponent?

Mafia elder statesman Joe Bonanno, aka Joe Bananas, had been boss of his own *borgata* for over thirty years when alliances on the Commission began to shift. Fearing those shifting alliances would prove unfavorable to him, Bonanno began to meddle in other families' affairs, trying to tip the scales in his favor.

Banana Republic is a nice clothing store, right? Long before the famous clothing store was started, "Banana Republic" was the term the United States government used for South and Central American countries where our CIA propped up leaders in order to control their governments, usually to ensure easy access to a single, lucrative crop, like bananas.

Joe Bonanno tried to pull off a typical CIA move, propping up another don to make his own Banana Republic out of another crime family. This wasn't why he was called Joe Bananas, but the name sure fits.

The other families got wind of Bonanno's intrigues and threw a monkey wrench into his plan; anyone friendly with Bonanno was vetoed as boss. But Bonanno didn't back down. Feeling even more threatened and outmaneuvered, he planned to take out the bosses of rival families in one fell swoop.

Before putting his plan into action, Bonanno approached Joseph

Magliocco, his chief candidate for boss of the family he wanted to control. Magliocco was to oversee the multi-hit contract that would elevate him to boss of his own family, but also relegate him to the role of Bonanno's puppet.

With dozens of loyal soldiers to choose from, Magliocco passed the contract on to a young follower named Joe Colombo. Colombo came across as a loyal henchman who'd do anything for his boss, but deep down he was burning with ambition. Years earlier, Colombo had displayed his acting ability when he feigned mental illness to get out of military duty. Colombo not only fooled the U.S. military but was such a good actor he snowed both the fledgling statesman Magliocco and the wily old fox, Bonanno.

Instead of loading up his guns and spilling the blood, Colombo loaded up his mouth and spilled the beans. He went directly to the other bosses and warned them of Bonanno and Magliocco's plans, requesting, in return for his betrayal, the top spot in his family.

Colombo was crowned don. Magliocco was happy to escape with his life, but the resultant pressure probably contributed to the massive heart attack that killed him a few months later. Bonanno's heart was made of stronger stuff; he took it on the lam and defied the Commission.

Colombo mastered the skills I spoke of earlier in "Why the Chin Wore Pajamas to Work." But a boss standing close enough to Colombo should have felt the heat from his burning ambition and figured out a way to neutralize him.

Years after Joe Bonanno retired, his Bonanno family was taken over by Mafia boss Joe Massino.

Massino had a knack for spotting and eliminating potential opponents.

Before Massino became boss, he was busy brown-nosing Philip "Rusty" Rastelli, then boss of the Bonanno family. While Rastelli was in prison, Massino became his eyes and ears on the street. Massino wasn't an Eagle Scout doing an old man favors; he was positioning himself for a grab at the crown when the old man croaked.

While Massino was baking cookies for Rastelli in prison, other wiseguys in the family were becoming dissatisfied with Rastelli's prison-based leadership, and decided to speak up. Three powerful capos led the opposition. Instead of a preemptive strike against Rastelli's loyalists, the three capos were willing to follow Mob protocol and air out their grievances at a sit-down with Massino.

Massino immediately began to conspire behind the scenes. While the sit was being arranged, he approached other families, asking permission to "protect Rastelli." Massino acted under the guise of a loyal knight defending his king. In truth, the three capos posed a direct threat to Massino, who couldn't wait to plop his fat ass on the throne. Massino then held two sits with the capos. At each sit, he humored them for political purposes; nothing was ever settled because Massino was unwilling to budge.

The third sit planned to resolve the capos' grievances would be their last. The three unarmed men walked up to the door and rang the doorbell of the 20/20 nightclub in Brooklyn, where the sit was scheduled to take place. They walked inside and greeted Massino, Dominick Napolitano, and Gerlando Sciascia—take note of these last two names; like Massino, they were men burning with ambition.

Normally, when you enter a home or social club, your host hangs your coat in the closet. But the closet was full—with four masked men armed with machine guns. They burst out, firing at the capos. Suffice to say, Joseph Massino was not a good host.

After the bodies were zipped up into canvas bags and buried, Massino, Napolitano, and Sciascia all shook hands. Mission accomplished. For now. Remember what I said—Massino had a knack for spotting potential opponents.

Many of the men who took part in these grisly murders would live out their lives: the shooters, the lookouts, and the burial squad.

Napolitano, however, was like Massino: an alpha male and charismatic leader. Massino, the master politician, knew it was unacceptable by Mob standards to kill Napolitano for this alone. He'd patiently wait for an opportunity to present itself.

When Napolitano screwed up by admitting undercover agent Joe Pistone into the Bonanno circle, Massino had the excuse he needed and ordered Napolitano's murder. When Napolitano's decomposed body was found, his fingers had been chewed off by wild animals. An appropriate end for a life lived in a jungle.

Gerlando Sciascia was the other ambitious man who helped Massino murder the three capos. Sciascia made his mistake when he told Massino that another wiseguy, Anthony Graziano, was using drugs, an insinuation that Graziano should be taken care of. Being "taken care of" in the Mob doesn't mean a reality TV show intervention—crime families don't tend to be supportive families.

Massino knew the fine line between a man who thinks he can manipulate the boss and a man who thinks he can be the boss.

Sciascia's burning ambition would burn no more. He took three shots to the head, had an eye shot out, and was dumped on the street, like trash.

> This is Joey [Massino] cleaning house.
> —FBI agent Charles Rooney answering FBI director
> Louis Freeh's inquiry into the Sciascia murder

Of the three ambitious men who planned and executed the murders of three other ambitious men, two were dead and Massino was left standing.

Massino could sniff out a potential opponent, arrange the politics in his favor or patiently await an excuse to act, then strike.

LESSON · 77

Don't Shoot a Rising Star:
Neutralizing Potential Opponents

MOB boss Johnny Torrio grew up during the Depression and is credited with starting the Chicago Outfit. At five feet three inches, Torrio proved that a big brain was far more important than a big body. For the better part of his life, he exhibited the rare ability to use reason in lieu of a gun, and never cheated his criminal partners. "There's plenty for everyone" was Torrio's motto.

Torrio had a gift for organization and was able to mold hoodlums into businessmen. One such hoodlum was the young Al Capone. When Torrio first recognized how smart and ambitious Capone was, he knew he had a problem. It wouldn't be long before Capone pushed Torrio aside or bumped him off. The usual Mob solution to this dilemma would be to kill Capone first. Didn't Massino kill every threat around him? But Torrio knew that Capone was worth much more to him alive than dead. What to do?

Torrio made Capone an offer he couldn't refuse: a partnership. Now, it may appear that Torrio was giving something up. Quite the contrary. Torrio found in Capone a man with whom he could expand his operations. Moreover, he neutralized a potential opponent. After many successful years together, Torrio retired and left the Windy City to Capone.

While Capone was in charge, Torrio still visited Chicago, and recommended new ideas. He and Capone became wealthy. Just as Torrio had predicted: "There was plenty for everyone."

Like Johnny Torrio, Sam Walton grew up during the rough and tumble times of the Depression. Walton possessed the same skills Torrio had, but applied them to legitimate business. Walton's first venture was a Ben Franklin variety store. The store was appropriately named since Walton emulated Benjamin Franklin's wit and wisdom.

After a successful run, Walton lost his lease for the variety store and had to close down. But Walton persevered, and soon opened another store, Walton's Five and Dime.

Like Torrio, Walton wanted to expand his operations. In doing so, he encountered smart and ambitious managers. One such manager was Willard Walker. Using a classic Torrio move, Walton neutralized Walker by offering him a piece of the action. Walker accepted.

Today, the kind of partnership Torrio and Walton struck with Capone and Walker is known as profit sharing.

Walton took on more and more partners, and eventually called his stores Walton's Family Center, and then just Walmart.

Sam Walton seems to have walked the straight and narrow, but in 2003, federal agents raided Walmart stores in twenty-one states and slapped them with a "racketeering" indictment, in which they were charged with violating U.S. labor laws.

James Linsey of Cohen, Weiss and Simon, a law firm representing the workers of Walmart, had this to say, "The essence of racketeering is layering so that you insulate the people at the top, whether it's Vito Corleone or Tony Soprano or, in this case, the top management of Walmart."

As noted earlier, we're all made of the same stuff.

LESSON 78

They Can Take It in the Ass on My Dance Floor: Don't Let Opinions Stand in the Way of Profit

THE Mafia bans gays from membership. As far as I know, they're not about to implement the "Don't Ask, Don't Tell" policy. However, the Mob will deal with anyone, without prejudice.

Some friends and I took over a nightclub in Manhattan. The former club owners catered to homosexuals one night a week. Before handing us the keys, they explained to us that gays were their best clientele.

"They're big spenders, and never cause any problems," said one owner. "I never have to worry about them wrecking the joint, and they don't sneak weapons in."

"They're our classiest clients," his partner added. "But I wouldn't care if they took it in the ass on my dance floor 'cause their cash is good."

As noted earlier in this book, the Mafia expects its members to adopt the values of the organization, and those who flout these values are dealt with swiftly and severely. That said, the Mafia does not question the values of others they do business with. Profit is the bottom line.

For a time, the Bonanno family allowed drugs while the other New York families did not. Still, all five families did business together. In contrast, U.S. businesspeople are often excluded from doing business in ripe markets because of political differences derived from conflicting values.

Well, who the fuck are we?

> The logic of criminal business, of the bosses, coincides with the most aggressive neoliberalism. The rules, dictated or imposed, are those of business, profit, and

victory over all the competition. Anything else is worthless. Anything else doesn't exist.

—Roberto Saviano, *Gomorrah*

Imagine a meeting where two Mafia bosses discuss millions of dollars, enough to enhance the riches of both families. The meeting goes well and a deal is hammered out. The two bosses shake hands and kiss. They walk outside to the parking lot where one don drives away in a big old '73 Caddy gas guzzler with a broken muffler, leaving a cloud of smoke behind. The other don, speaking through a cough, announces to his men that he's canceling the deal. His reason: the don in the Caddy is polluting the world.

The next thing to pollute that parking lot would be gun smoke; the don who canceled the deal would be dead.

It's naive to think that your values should be universal.

If you want to fix the world, and plan to shun everyone who doesn't agree with your ideas of right and wrong, you're cutting off your nose to spite your face. If you lose a little sleep over some of the characters you deal with, donate some of your profits toward bettering the world.

If the Mafia had imposed economic sanctions on countries like Cuba, India, South Africa, Iran, and Iraq, then the infamous Pizza Connection, in which the Mafia dominated the global drug trade, would never have connected.

It's important to stay connected with our world. Teach people by example.

In ancient times, a Greek historian named Herodotus traveled the known world recording stories for
his book, *The Histories.*

Back then, most nations were run like Mafia
fiefdoms, ruled by dictators who make today's Mob

bosses look like Tinker Bells. Persia, or modern-day Iran, was one such nation.

In *The Histories*, Herodotus writes of a Persian king named Darius who ruled over various ethnic groups within his kingdom. One day, "Don" Darius called on a bunch of Greeks within his realm and said to them, "I know youse cremate your parents when they die, but how much would I have to pay youse to eat them instead?"

The Greeks took offense and told Darius, in so many words, to go fuck himself.

Darius then called on a bunch of Indians within his realm and said to them, "I know youse eat your parents when they die, but how much would I have to pay youse to cremate them instead?"

The Indians were appalled and answered Darius in the same manner as the Greeks.

Based on Darius's inquiry, Herodotus concluded that societies have different customs and therefore reasoned that right and wrong are subjective.

LESSON 79

Choosing Your Consigliere

IN the early days of the American Mafia, a consigliere, or counselor of a family, was an older man chosen for his experience, wisdom, and street smarts. He was well respected and counted upon to remain objective in all of his decisions. A skilled diplomat, he could defuse potential problems and advise the boss on how to steer the family around obstacles.

Over time, however, this revered position became a political one, and the consigliere amounted to the number-three man in the family in terms of wealth and power.

Sammy "The Bull" Gravano, before being elevated to the position of underboss, was appointed consigliere of the Gambino family at the tender age of forty. Gravano held court over men twice his age and ten times as smart. The older wiseguys listened to his decisions, not on account of any accrued wisdom, but because he'd kill them if they didn't. The Mob neglected to honor the true purpose of this position, and paid a heavy price.

In business, you need a good consigliere, someone you trust to give sound advice. That someone should be rooting for your success, but detached from your business and therefore able to see things clearly. A spouse, a sibling, a mentor—pick a person who can be trusted, and you'll have a great source to turn to for advice.

LESSON 80

Why Frankie Fever Don't Believe the Hype

A capo named Frankie Fever once told me a story about his early years on the street. He was a teenager, sitting in a pizzeria eating a slice, when two guys walked in and sat down at a table behind him. One guy said to the other, "I got five grand together, can you give it to me for five?"

The other guy said, "No way, you can flip this shit for twelve anywhere. I gotta get six."

"I can't do it," said the first guy. "Five is all I got. Can you give it to me on the arm? I'll square up with you after I sell it."

"No way," said the second guy.

"I'll see what I can do." The first guy got up and walked out of the pizzeria.

Frankie turned around in his seat to face the guy still sitting there and said, "Whatchu got?"

"Ten pounds of *skunk* weed. It goes for twelve grand. You interested?"

"You lookin' for six?" asked Frankie.

"Yeah."

Frankie knew that skunk was marijuana, but knew little else about the drug trade. He did know if he got six grand together, he could double his money on the street.

"I'll be back in twenty minutes," said Frankie. "Hold it for me."

"Hurry up. If my friend comes back with the cash, I gotta let it go."

Frankie had two grand of his own. He ran down the block to his future father-in-law's house and asked to borrow the other four, promising him five in return. Frankie then ran back to the pizzeria and made the buy.

Ten minutes later, Frankie was sitting at home wondering what to do with ten pounds of compressed oregano. He'd been duped. He never saw the guys again.

Frankie told me he learned two major lessons that day. Never jump at anything—as we've already covered in "Fireproof Your Ass"—and don't buy something just because someone else wants it.

As crazy as it may sound, this is how Hollywood and the publishing industry works. A book or screenplay can float around forever, but if one or more people suddenly want it, there's a buzz and everyone starts to bid, pumping up the price.

Major publishers and film studios write off losing propositions. You, however, should never bid on or buy something just because someone else wants it.

LESSON 81

I Got an Inside Guy: Staying Up on the Competition

MY fence once told me, "If a company has five hundred employees, half are ripe for an inside tip."

Imagine going into a conference room and knowing exactly what the other party wants or needs to get out of the negotiations—their rock-bottom price, the most they'll give, the least they'll take. That info can all be provided to you over a beer at Patrick's Pub.

When pulling off heists, my biggest tips came from ordinary employees, an inside guy or gal privy to golden information.

Every company has its share of people willing to talk. I can't count how many times I sat in a diner booth whispering with an inside guy as he arranged table napkins as buildings, coffee mugs as trucks, and forks as people.

Sure, a lot of these tipsters were backed up on their bills, behind on the rent, or drowning in credit card debt. But sometimes, my inside guy didn't even want a cut from the take; he just wanted to talk over a drink.

People are lonely and many are unhappy with the company they work for. Beer, wine, or a cocktail will loosen people's screws, but most people will talk if you're just willing to listen.

LESSON 82

Hide Your Money Under the Mattress: Stay Cash Heavy

I knew a fence named Freddie. Besides moving stolen goods, Freddie was involved in a million other scams. If Freddie got jammed up on the street and owed some coin, he'd hem and haw until the other guy called for a sit-down.

At the sit, Freddie would admit to the debt but claim he was broke. As a gesture of good faith, he'd offer to pay even more than he owed, but in merchandise, of which he had plenty lying around. In this way, Freddie didn't make many friends, but he stayed cash heavy and unloaded goods he wanted to sell anyhow.

A company should avoid Freddie's habit of alienating people but adopt his strategy of holding on to cash.

The capricious way of the streets has ingrained in mobsters the hard truth that today's income, however secure it may seem, can be cut off tomorrow. The Mob offers no pension, severance package, or 401(k). It's all about how much cash you can stash, which is not such a bad goal for anybody, as we have seen in recent economic times.

Most of a mobster's criminal affairs are cash transactions, so staying cash heavy is deeply rooted in his behavior. When a mobster goes into business, he brings his cash-heavy mind-set with him. Thrust into an office, he finds himself juggling phone calls, customers, credit cards, insurance policies, stocks, bonds, bank accounts, and payroll. But he never forgets, as so many businesspeople do, that cash flow must remain his primary concern at all times.

Big companies need massive credit to survive in the corporate jungle, but keep a heavy cash reserve behind your outstanding debt. During the latest economic crunch, companies with huge cash reserves survived. So did the Mafia—without bailout money.

LESSON 83

Poverty Sucks. Or Does It?

IN the Mob, when shit hits the fan, you're in the wind.

While on the run, it's not the chase that bothers you—that's exciting. It's being out of touch with loved ones. Even if I was staying at a five-star hotel, I'd get tired of living out of a suitcase, and long for a home-cooked meal. But that's The Life. You tough it out, or it breaks you.

While on the lam with other mobsters, I could see who was built for hardships and who wasn't, who could survive a stint in jail and who'd probably fold under pressure.

You don't have to experience life on the lam or serve a prison sentence to prepare yourself for a tough spell that's bound to happen now and then. You just have to remember where you came from. If you become a big shot and forget your roots, your background is useless.

On the other hand, a leader who never forgets what it's like to have little or nothing can survive any hardship.

> He will always be a slave who does not know how to live upon a little.
>
> —Horace

Sicilian Mob boss Bernardo Provenzano never forgot his peasant background. When fate allowed, Provenzano lived in a mansion by the sea, wore the finest clothes, and drove the fastest cars. However, when the need arose, Provenzano traded in his fancy clothes for a farmer's outfit, and his resort-style digs for a dive in the boonies. He'd recall his ragged roots, the memory of which enabled him to tough it out while maintaining control of his men and, more important, himself.

When the law finally pinched Provenzano, the shabby cottage he was living in stank of stale cheese and rotten vegetables.

Mob boss Frank Costello slept inside a vat on his way to America. Carlo Gambino braved the choppy transatlantic crossing as a stowaway. Both men never forgot their roots.

If you're reading this book, chances are you come from humble origins. Never forget it!

> The most successful CEOs do often have a certain make-up—often they come from adversity, having had a difficult background in some way that has helped to create the DNA of a super-CEO.
> —Steve Tappin, author of *The Secrets of CEOs*

A leader willing to face problems head-on, take a salary cut, and sacrifice personal time and energy is a leader worth following.

Poverty doesn't always suck. If you remember what it was like, that memory will carry you through even the hardest times.

LESSON 84

The Mafia Is a Brand Name: When to Franchise

ONE reason a Mafia associate works so hard to get in with a family is because once he's in, he has the potential to earn much more using the family name.

Pete Penovich was a Chicago gambling boss during the time of Al Capone. At Capone's criminal trial, Penovich testified that he voluntarily gave up 100 percent of his own profitable gambling machine when he was offered 25 percent to throw in with Capone's Outfit. Penovich said that the original 25 was later cut down to 5 percent. Yet he was never forced to stay with the Outfit, and earned more at 5 percent under the Capone franchise than he had earned alone.

The Capone gambling franchise offered Penovich a larger clientele, better locations, and strong protection.

For similar reasons, Aunt Mary's Coffee Shop might convert to a Starbucks.

Think about it.

LESSON 85

It's Good to Be King: But No One Is Above the Law

LONG before there was John Gotti of Queens, who considered himself a king, there was King John of England, who considered himself a don.

June 15, 1215. A sit-down was arranged at Runnymede near Windsor Castle in England. King John was about to meet with his barons, or capos. By this time, everyone in the realm was disgusted with the king's horseshit; he thought he was above the law. The barons could have easily whacked him but instead they gave him an ultimatum.

They told their king that he ruled by their consent and was therefore bound by the same rules as everyone else. They also made it clear to him that if he broke any rules, they were going to whack him. King John got the message.

Four hundred years later, in 1649, King Charles I of England ignored the rules and his capos chopped off his head. They don't fuck around in England.

> My father always said . . . if you break the rules, you end up in a dumpster. If I break rules, meaning himself, they're gonna put two in my hat and put me in a dumpster. That's the way it works.
>
> —John Gotti, Jr., quoting his father, John Gotti, Sr.

A Lucchese mobster once told me, "The family belongs to us. We put our boss there, an' we can take him down."

How often do leaders slip into the delusion that they're above the rules?

Usually, the body of a Mafia don drops along with his approval rating. This danger keeps most bosses in line.

> Colombo had to go because he . . . believed he was bigger than the mob, that he was indestructible. Wrong.
> —Joey Black

You might think, Well, I'm not a Mob boss, no one's going to shoot me. Think again. Plenty of employees go postal. You're also not immune to employee discontent. A petty employee might break the pencil sharpener or water cooler, steal the pens and pencils. No big deal. What about the employee who gives away company secrets, that inside guy I spoke about earlier? Every company has its share of jerks, you can't help that. But if you're disliked, you risk a consensus of enemies.

Al Capone was liked by his employees. He owned a piece of an Italian restaurant where a rival mobster, Joseph Aiello, offered ten grand to the chef to sprinkle a little poison over Capone's pasta instead of parmesan cheese. The chef, who liked Capone, went straight to Big Al and told him about the plot.

> I liked running booze for Dean. He paid well; he never stiffed his drivers. . . . He really believed in treating his people well.
> —Employee of Chicago mobster Dean O'Banion, quoted in T. J. English, *Paddy Whacked*

Unlike Capone, Aiello's employees weren't very fond of him. He died with thirty holes in him, about the same amount of holes on a parmesan cheese grater, the instrument that might've killed Capone if he hadn't been so well liked.

LESSON 86

Guys Like Us, Guys Like Them:
Stick with What You Know

ONE day I was bullshitting with another mobster when we heard over the radio that the space shuttle had landed safely.

"Fuckin' amazing," I said. "Imagine the brains it takes to get that fuckin' thing into space and back."

Nonchalantly, he replied, "They got guys like us for this. They got guys like them for that."

His was a brilliant statement in all of its simplicity. The world has people cut out for all different things. Together, we make the Earth go round.

Al Capone called the stock market a "racket" and knew enough to stay out of it. But most people aren't as realistic about their limits as Capone.

I knew a guy on the street I'll call Bobby. Bobby knew mobsters all his life, might've exchanged a couple of favors with them over the years, but for the most part, he was legit. Through hard work, Bobby built up a successful private sanitation business. Like any smart businessman who accumulates wealth, Bobby dabbled in real estate.

As a landlord, Bobby rented out a building to a restaurateur. The restaurant failed and the owner abandoned the lease but left behind the ovens, tables, and a nicely decorated place. Instead of renting the building to someone new, Bobby took over the restaurant. He hired a top-notch chef and began to advertise.

Bobby knew that mobsters are big spenders, so he invited all the mobsters he knew to his place. Although Bobby was a little out of his realm, he pulled it off; the restaurant was packed.

So far, no mistakes. Bobby had spotted an opportunity and turned garbage into gold. His wealth and reputation increased.

Next, Bobby stepped into a realm he knew nothing about.

All day and night, Bobby rubbed shoulders with mobsters. Soon, they rubbed off on him, and Bobby began to think of himself as a mobster. After all, he was rich, he could live out any fantasy, right?

Bobby raised the floor in a corner of his restaurant and put an oval table with a telephone there. Every night during dinner, patrons could see Bobby dressed in pin-striped suits with silk hankies, dialing or answering the phone. All he needed was a fluffy white cat on his lap.

Knowing that real wiseguys often ate there, young Mob wannabes began to frequent the place. When the real wiseguys shunned them, Bobby saw an opportunity to mobilize the rejects and form his own crew.

Soon, the wannabes were pulling off scores and bringing Bobby an end.

Here's a guy worth millions, who abandons a thriving sanitation business to accept a measly case of scotch from a stolen liquor truck here, or a crate of swag cigarettes there. He even left his wife for a bimbo.

When the feds found out that Bobby's restaurant was a Mafia hot spot, they set up surveillance cameras across the street. Bobby then did what any Mafia big shot would do, who really isn't a Mafia big shot, and really didn't know what the fuck he was doing. He ordered his crew of misfits to burn down the building where the FBI had set up their cameras. This act is equivalent to entering the J. Edgar Hoover building in Washington, D.C., walking straight up to the FBI director, and spitting in his face.

Unfortunately for Bobby, the FBI director was indeed an FBI director, not someone who was pretending. The feds nailed Bobby's ass to the wall. One by one, they turned his all-star cast of idiots into stool pigeons, closed down his restaurant, and slapped him with a multi-count racketeering indictment.

Bobby lost his wife, his kids, his sanitation business, and his freedom. And for what? To play wiseguy.

How many rich businessmen think their wealth translates into wisdom, and believe they can master any field and live out any fantasy?

Bobby's mistake isn't unique; it's an error repeated throughout history.

During the days of ancient Rome, a guy named Crassus had a genius for business affairs and became filthy rich. Financial success convinced Crassus that he could conquer any field, even a battlefield.

With no experience in warfare, Crassus set out to conquer the Parthian Empire. He dismissed the warnings of experienced generals because, after all, he was rich and they weren't. Instead of dying a proud, wealthy man, sipping a martini while getting a blowjob, Crassus died in shame, brutally murdered at the hands of his enemies. He also dragged thirty thousand legionnaires into the grave with him.

Didn't Bobby drag his family and employees down with him?

Stick to what you know.

Marcus Aurelius Was a Great Emperor, but That Doesn't
Mean His Son Was: The Perils of Nepotism

WHEN making a historical drama, Hollywood will happily sacrifice accuracy to jazz up a film. The film *Gladiator*, starring Russell
Crowe, was no different, except the filmmakers were spot-on portray-
ing Marcus Aurelius as a great Roman emperor and his son Commodus as a total loser.

The real-life Marcus Aurelius kept a personal notebook we now
call the *Meditations*, which serves as a practical guide to living in a
crazy world. As old as it is, the book applies perfectly today because,
as you've learned, human nature is constant.

In the opening pages of the *Meditations*, Marcus Aurelius thanks
his family and friends for what they've taught him: "From my grand-
father, good morals; my father, modesty; my mother, piety; my gover-
nor, hard labor . . ." The list goes on.

Marcus Aurelius didn't write about the unpleasant things he
received from people, like the agita he got from his son, Commodus.
He passed on that agita to the Roman people when he allowed the
bum to assume his throne. Commodus abandoned himself to a life
of luxury and sexual depravity. Instead of governing the empire, he
was fighting in the Colosseum or throwing wild orgies. His hands-off
approach to governing left the empire spiraling out of control.

Marcus Aurelius made a major mistake some Mob bosses have
repeated, and others have wisely avoided.

For a long time, Bernardo Provenzano shared leadership of the
Sicilian Mafia with Totò Riina. Provenzano and Riina came from the
same peasant stock. Both were born and raised in the Sicilian village of
Corleone. They began their criminal careers around the same time and

suffered similar ups and downs on their way up the Mafia ladder. They reached the top together, and became corulers of a billion-dollar empire.

Provenzano was a mild-mannered man who offered sound advice to his followers and often counseled peace. Many of his men referred to him as "The Philosopher." Riina, on the other hand, was quick to kill, and his men nicknamed him "The Beast."

Provenzano and Riina each had two sons but, given their respective nicknames, it's not surprising that only one of them was able to accurately assess his son's potential.

> [Provenzano] was worried his sons might become part of Cosa Nostra. He wanted to stop this happening before it was too late.
> —Chief anti-Mafia prosecutor Pietro Grasso

Provenzano knew that his sons, raised under far different circumstances than he had been, were totally unequipped to inhabit, much less rule, the treacherous world of La Cosa Nostra. Thus, he kept them far away from the family business, assessed their attributes, and guided them toward appropriate career paths. Both went to university and pursued respectable careers.

While Provenzano was pushing his sons away from organized crime, Riina was drawing his own sons closer. When Riina was sent to prison for life, he appointed his older son, Giovanni, as don.

As corulers of the Sicilian Mafia, the Philosopher and the Beast complemented each other; their combination of attributes was the recipe for success. Giovanni, however, was all beast like his father. With no one to temper his brutality, he launched a bloody reign. Unfit to rule, he received a dozen life sentences by age twenty-four.

> I started learning about guns when I was six . . . my father also taught me . . . to aim for the head and get off at least two bullets.
> —Albert DeMeo, son of Mafia hit man Roy DeMeo

The difficulties of ruling Italy during the time of Marcus Aurelius, or ruling Italy's underworld during the time of Provenzano and Riina, were very similar. The job required a peculiar character, born of unique experiences.

> I rule with my head.
>
> —Bernardo Provenzano

Your kids, being raised in a successful household, have a different set of experiences that may not make them well suited to your path.

Still, if you think your son or daughter can run your business, and you're willing to subject them to the stress of leadership, go for it. But make that decision with your head, like Bernardo Provenzano, not your heart.

LESSON 88

Leave the Gun, Take the Cannolis . . . and
Beware of Hubris

WHEN I left the Mob, I left the bad things behind—the gun—
and kept the sweet things I'd picked up along the way—the cannolis.
This gun-cannoli formula, which involves looking back at our past,
can be instrumental in helping anyone change for the better.

Not one moment of our lives, even those moments we prefer
to forget, has been for naught if we analyze and learn from each of
our experiences. And the wealth of wisdom our past can provide is
demonstrative of the universal lessons we can glean from a broad
study of history.

Throughout this book, I pointed out the striking similarities
between historical events and situations we encounter every day. I
sometimes mentioned the ancient Greeks. In addition to everything
else the Greeks have taught us, they pointed out the successful man's
propensity to gloat. Having attained wealth and power, leaders from
all walks of life often exhibit outrageous pride and arrogance. Convinced of their own brilliance, they dismiss rational advice or refuse
advice altogether. This, the Greeks called hubris.

Since a leader's decisions affect so many, his hubris will also
imperil many. Should you reach the top, I'll warn you now that it is
there you will have to confront your most formidable opponent—
yourself. This brings me to one final lesson in which I'll draw a
remarkable comparison between three different leaders: the head of
a nation, the boss of a Mafia family, and a CEO, each of whom suffered from hubris.

During his reign, Adolf Hitler proudly proclaimed, "I am Fuhrer
of a Reich *that will last for a thousand years."* Hitler's "thousand-year

Reich" lasted twelve years, and his German nation was destroyed along with it.

During his reign, John Gotti was caught on audiotape proudly proclaiming, "This is gonna be a Cosa Nostra till I die. Be it an hour from now, or be it tonight, or *a hundred years from now."*

Gotti's "hundred-year Cosa Nostra" was in disarray less than two years after this tape was recorded. His Gambino family was dismantled by informants and never again achieved its prominent influence.

During his reign, CEO Kenneth Lay sent an e-mail to his employees saying, "We have the *finest organization in American business today."*

Lay's "finest organization," Enron, collapsed less than four months after this e-mail was sent. The company's destruction was so fast and total that twenty thousand employees were given thirty minutes to clean out their desks. Lay was picked up on federal charges and convicted in criminal court, just like Gotti.

> The pride of your heart has deceived you, you who live in
> the clefts of the rocks, who occupy the heights of the hill.
> Though you build your nest as high as the eagle's, from
> there I will bring you down, declares the Lord.
>
> —Jeremiah 49:16

Hitler, Gotti, and Lay all clawed their way up the ladder but got dizzy with success and suffered from hubris.

Always remember, it can take you years to get to the top but less than a minute to fall. The Empire State Building has 1,860 steps that would take a fit person thirty minutes to climb. A fall from the top takes a matter of seconds—unless you're Superman and can fly. You're not Superman. And that's the point.

After you achieve that success you've dreamed of, beware of hubris.

EPILOGUE

Be a Pizza Egg Roll

FEW men in the Mob have actually read Machiavelli's *The Prince,* but nearly every wiseguy prides himself on being "Machiavellian." They have an idea that "Machiavellian" means to conquer men "by force and by fraud," and that appeals to them.

I've read Niccolò Machiavelli's *The Prince*, and it's discouraging to see that so many of today's business books have basically repackaged what Machiavelli wrote five hundred years ago and, by doing so, led people down the wrong path in life. Today's lack of ethics in business can be traced, in part, to these contemporary imitations.

Machiavelli was accurate in his assessment of human flaws, but life's journey should include a daily struggle against our base impulse to succeed at any cost. We can't simply surrender to our primitive instincts, as Machiavelli suggests.

Machiavelli tells us to gain and keep the upper hand by any means, that there's no such thing as justice, honor, or integrity, and that morality should play no part in our dealings, unless we're pretending. But Machiavelli failed to address that little idea called karma.

I've been up close and personal with men who've held immense power, and I've had considerable power in my own hands; my experiences prove that there are undeniable consequences to our actions. By omitting this central fact, Machiavelli may be responsible for the great fortunes of a dozen or so men and women who were completely numb to the welfare of others, and the misfortunes of millions who eat, sleep, and breathe like the rest of us.

While Machiavelli's instruction may help you achieve success in business or politics, it guarantees your failure in other aspects of life, leaving you with no friends and relatives who hate you. Rich but poor. Successful but sad. Social but lonely. Is this what you want? Money and power at any cost?

Machiavelli's advice may help you attain great heights, but you'll find it very lonely at the top, living the life of a miserable fuck who suffers from paranoia, sleepless nights, and pangs of conscience. These ailments will eventually wear you down, one way or another.

I've sat beside Mob bosses at the height of their power, and shared the same cockroach-infested cells with them after they were stripped of that power. Alone, in private conversation, some have confessed their regrets to me. One, in particular, told me that his exalted position on the street made the pain of prison that much worse. This brought to mind a passage I'd read in Caesar's autobiography in which he said, "When the immortal gods wish to punish a guilty man, they often grant him all the more prosperity, all the longer impunity, simply that he may suffer the more when his good fortune is reversed."

You may know Machiavellian businesspeople who appear successful. Are you privy to their private lives? Can you see tomorrow? All that we do, good and bad, is repaid in kind.

Confucius was a Chinese philosopher who counseled wisdom, justice, and moderation. He told leaders to rule, not by force, but by virtue. His philosophy is the polar opposite of Machiavelli's.

> Virtue's a thing that none can take away, but money changes owners all day.
>
> —Plutarch, *Life of Solon*

I advise you to read Machiavelli's *The Prince* for an understanding of how low your competitors may stoop, and then rise above the muck and follow the path of Confucius. Be a pizza egg roll.

Have true goals. Treat people with dignity. And strive to make our world a better place. I assure you, you can do this and get rich in the process, for wealth, without wisdom, is wasted.

ACKNOWLEDGMENTS

A special thanks to my friend Harry Stein. Harry and I often talked about my life in the Mafia and he suggested that many of the stories I shared with him would make an interesting book. Another special thanks to Nick Pileggi, a true man of honor in every way.

To my father, my stepmother, Betty, my sister, Lisa, and my brother-in-law, Ralph; my cousins Donald and Debbie, Denise and John; my Uncle Anthony and Aunt Claudette; Fat George, Rita, Norma and Jerry, Donna C., Louis and his father-in-law, Richie, Ronnie and Tish. Thank you all for being there for me during those horrible years in a prison cell.

To John "Johnny Parkway" Brunetti, David Black, Tommy Gallagher, Robin Shamburg, Ruda Dauphin, Rabbi Arthur Rulnick, Marshall and Sandy Rulnick, Paul and Karen Dawson, Burt and Suzy Farbman, and Bill Yosses.

To Mario the Gardener and his brother, John. Dave Berman, John Farrar, Tim Shaw, Billy Rothar, Beth Birnbaum, Kieran and Sarah McLoughlin, Renee Queen, Charles and Joseph Lamberta, Edward Kanaley, Vic Orena, Jr., Michael Sessa, and Markos Pappas.

To Kevin Van Name, who stood up and served a stint in prison, went straight, and opened up Harrison House, a place where alcoholics and drug addicts are put on the right path.

Acknowledgments

Thanks to the late Jerry Bauer, Rhoda Pobliner, and Richard Messina, who died in prison—thank you for everything you taught me, Richard.

To the generous W. Dahveed Rubin, who sent me my first complete edition of *The Babylonian Talmud*.

To my friend and agent, Lisa Queen, and my editors at Portfolio, Emily Angell, David Moldawer, and Adrian Zackheim.

To my love, Gabriella, who is more beautiful every day.

To my mother, Jo Ann, who worked so hard and taught me so much but never saw the fruits of her labor.

And to Almighty God, who, in a dark and lonely prison cell, opened my eyes.

NOTES

vii **The organization chart**: Roy Rowan, "The Fifty Biggest Mafia Bosses," *Fortune,* November 10, 1986, pp. 24–35.

xix **A career of banditry**: Edgar Snow, *Red Star over China: The Classic Account of the Birth of Chinese Communism,* First Revised and Enlarged Edition (New York: Grove Press, 1968), p. 44.

xxii **We only kill**: Carl Sifakis, *The Mafia Encyclopedia: From Accardo to Zwillman,* Third Edition (New York: Checkmark Books, 2005), p. 418.

xxii **Jonathan Swift**: Jacques Barzun, *From Dawn to Decadence: 1500 to the Present: 500, Years of Western Cultural Life* (New York: HarperCollins, 2000), p. 328.

xxii **Whereas I, lost**: Pierre de Beaumarchais, *The Marriage of Figaro,* trans. John Wood (New York: Penguin Books, 2004), p. 199.

xxiii **There are now**: Louis Antoine Fauvelet de Bourrienne, *Memoirs of Napoleon Bonaparte,* New and Revised Edition, ed. R. W. Phipps, Volume 1 (New York: Charles Scribner's Sons, 1891), p. 401.

1 **Mr. Persico . . . you are**: Selwyn Raab, *Five Families: The Rise, Decline, and Resurgence of America's Most Powerful Mafia Empires* (New York: Thomas Dunne Books, 2005), p. 348.

2 **His intelligence and personality**: John Marzulli, "Colombo Boss Alphonse (Allie Boy) Persico Sentenced to Life in Prison for 1999 Hit," *New York Daily News,* February 27, 2009.

2 **Mafia families are cut**: Pino Arlacchi, *Mafia Business: The Mafia Ethic and the Spirit of Capitalism,* trans. Martin Ryle (London: Verso, 1987), p. 136.

3 **Some of them, except**: *Godfathers Collection: The True History of the Mafia,* Volume One, DVD, A&E Home Video/The History Channel, 2004.

4 **"Today, the power"**: "Remarks Announcing Federal Initiatives Against Drug Trafficking and Organized Crime." Speech given by President Ronald Reagan, October 14, 1982, www.reagan.utexas.edu/archives/speeches/1982/101482c.htm.

4 **These criminal gangs**: Kefauver Committee Interim Report #2, February 28, 1951, U.S. Senate Special Committee to Investigate Organized Crime in Interstate Commerce.

5 **"[Petrizzo] was one of"**: Selwyn Raab, "Double Portrait of a Man on Trial Astounds Friends." *New York Times,* April 11, 1995.

Notes

5 **My word is better:** Selwyn Raab, *Five Families: The Rise, Decline, and Resurgence of America's Most Powerful Mafia Empires* (New York: Thomas Dunne Books, 2005), p. 335.

5 **the IBM Building, South Street:** Selwyn Raab, "Double Portrait of a Man on Trial Astounds Friends," *New York Times,* April 11, 1995.

5 **The success of the:** Nicholas Pileggi, "The Mafia Is Good for You," *The Saturday Evening Post,* November 30, 1968, p. 18.

7 **Good morning, gentlemen:** Curt Gentry, *J. Edgar Hoover: The Man and the Secrets* (New York: Plume, 1992), p. 457.

10 **[Chris] Rosenberg was a:** *Mobsters: Roy DeMeo, Part 2: No Turning Back,* The Biography Channel, 2009.

11 **We can't be letting:** Philip Carlo, *The Ice Man: Confessions of a Mafia Contract Killer* (New York: St. Martin's Press, 2006), p. 62.

13 **The thing you've got:** Nicholas Pileggi, *Wise Guy: Life in a Mafia Family* (New York: Pocket Books, 1987), p. 96.

14 **I'm going to a:** Selwyn Raab, *Five Families: The Rise, Decline, and Resurgence of America's Most Powerful Mafia Empires* (New York: Thomas Dunne Books, 2005), p. 616.

18 **But tell me, Charlie:** Martin A. Gosch and Richard Hammer, *The Last Testament of Lucky Luciano* (Boston: Little, Brown, and Company, 1975), p. 116.

18 **Soldier: "My business is":** Gene Mustain and Jerry Capeci, *Murder Machine: A True Story of Murder, Madness, and the Mafia* (New York: Onyx, 1993), p. 111.

19 **Trust your memory:** Dennis Eisenberg, Uri Dan, and Eli Landau, *Meyer Lansky: Mogul of the Mob* (New York: Paddington Press, 1979), p. 108.

20 **It would have been:** Nicholas Pileggi, *Casino: Love and Honor in Las Vegas* (New York: Simon & Schuster, 1995), p. 149.

20 **A large mass of recent:** Geoff Colvin, *Talent Is Overrated: What Really Separates World-Class Performers from Everybody Else* (New York: Portfolio, 2008), p. 45.

21 **War is a very rough:** Robert Dallek, *Nixon and Kissinger: Partners in Power* (New York: HarperCollins, 2007), p. 135.

22 **Louie [Milito] knew:** Peter Maas, *Underboss: Sammy the Bull Gravano's Story of Life in the Mafia* (New York: HarperTorch, 1997), p. 397.

24 **I've never broken:** Lawrence H. Larsen and Nancy J. Hulston, *Pendergast!* (Columbia: University of Missouri Press, 1997), p. 184.

24 **"We made an":** Peter Maas, *Underboss: Sammy the Bull Gravano's Story of Life in the Mafia* (New York: HarperTorch, 1997), p. 327.

25 **I told you I'd:** Carl Sifakis, *The Mafia Encyclopedia: From Accardo to Zwillman,* Third Edition (New York: Checkmark Books, 2005), p. 144.

26 **[Paul Castellano] is a greedy:** Philip Carlo, *Gaspipe: Confessions of a Mafia Boss* (New York: Harper, 2009), p. 137.

26 **"On the patties":** Jonathan Kwitny, *Vicious Circles: The Mafia in the Marketplace* (New York: W.W. Norton & Company, 1979), p. 14.

27 **"twelve pounds of":** William L. Shirer, *The Rise and Fall of the Third Reich: A History of Nazi Germany* (New York: MJF Books, 1988), p. 971.

27 **For putting bodies:** Ibid.

30 **Jimmy lived in:** Louis Ferrante, *Unlocked: The Life and Crimes of a Mafia Insider* (New York: Harper Paperbacks, 2009), p. 23.

31 **OC [organized crime] has become a:** Mike La Sorte, "Defining Organized Crime," AmericanMafia.com Features article 349, May 2006.

32 **The fact of having:** Salvatore Lupo, *La Storia della Mafia*, in Clare Longrigg, *Boss of Bosses: A Journey Into the Heart of the Sicilian Mafia* (New York: Thomas Dunne Books, 2008), p. 67.

34   **I thought of:** Frank Sinatra, "That's Life," by Dean Kay and Kelly Gordon, recorded October 18, 1966.

35   **Eradication of organized:** *Mafia Empire,* DVD, Mpi Home Video, 2006.

35   **I am just a:** Selwyn Raab, *Five Families: The Rise, Decline, and Resurgence of America's Most Powerful Mafia Empires* (New York: Thomas Dunne Books, 2005), p. 42.

36   **Organized crime goes:** Ibid., p. 707.

37   **Flexibility and durability:** *Mafia Empire,* DVD, Mpi Home Video, 2006.

38   **A hard worker:** John H. Davis, *Mafia Kingfish: Carlos Marcello and the Assassination of John F. Kennedy* (New York: Signet, 1989), p. 77.

38   **It's not that he:** Clare Longrigg, *Boss of Bosses: A Journey into the Heart of the Sicilian Mafia* (New York: Thomas Dunne Books, 2008), p. 154.

39   **"They were almost":** *Mafia Empire,* DVD, Mpi Home Video, 2006.

40   **Brutus drove his:** Adrian Goldsworthy, *Caesar: Life of a Colossus* (New Haven, CT: Yale University Press, 2006), p. 509.

41   **Pietro was discovered:** From *Mafia Wars: The Confessions of Tommaso Buscetta,* by Tim Shawcross and Martin Young, in *The Mammoth Book of the Mafia,* eds. Nigel and Colin Cawthorne (Philadelphia: Running Press, 2009), p. 320.

43   **Meyer Lansky outlived:** *Godfathers Collection: The True History of the Mafia,* Volume Two, DVD, A&E Home Video/The History Channel, 2004.

45   **Words can raise:** Aristophanes, *The Birds,* in *Aristophanes: The Complete Plays,* trans. Paul Roche (New York: New American Library, 2005). p. 401.

46   **Practice elocution:** F. Scott Fitzgerald, *The Great Gatsby* (New York: Scribner Paperback Fiction, 1995), p. 181.

46   **The greatest regret:** Joseph Bonanno and Sergio Lalli, *A Man of Honor: The Autobiography of Joseph Bonanno* (New York: St. Martin's Paperbacks, 1983), p. 382.

47   **When push comes:** Sam Giancana and Chuck Giancana, *Double Cross: The Explosive, Inside Story of the Mobster Who Controlled America* (New York: Warner Books, 1992), p. 185.

47   **Going to trial:** Hunter S. Thompson, *Song of the Doomed: More Notes on the Death of the American Dream* (New York: Simon & Schuster, 2002), p. 353.

48   **When I was:** Antony Thomas, *Rhodes: The Race for Africa* (London: BBC Books, 1996), p. 296.

50   **Tony [Spilotro] was:** Nicholas Pileggi, *Casino: Love and Honor in Las Vegas* (New York: Simon & Schuster, 1995), pp. 148–49.

50   **another bickering Europe:** James Thomas Flexner, *Washington: The Indispensable Man* (Boston: Little, Brown, and Company, 1974), p. 288.

52   **[Lucky] Luciano had:** Selwyn Raab, *Five Families: The Rise, Decline, and Resurgence of America's Most Powerful Mafia Empires* (New York: Thomas Dunne Books, 2005), p. 77.

53   **The Genovese family is:** *Godfathers Collection: The True History of the Mafia,* Volume Two, DVD, A&E Home Video/The History Channel, 2004.

53   **Bonasera: How much shall I:** Mario Puzo *The Godfather* (New York: G.P. Putnam's Sons, 1969), pp. 32-33.

54   **Favors are like:** Nelson DeMille, *The Gold Coast* (New York: Warner Books, 2006), p. 594.

59   **"Stalin became the":** Simon Sebag Montefiore, *Young Stalin* (London: Phoenix, 2008), p. 205.

59   **"I have seen him":** Nikita Khrushchev, *Khrushchev Remembers,* trans. and ed. Strobe Talbott (Boston: Little, Brown, 1970), p. xiii.

59   **Most of these guys:** Joseph D. Pistone and Richard Woodley, *Donnie Brasco: My Undercover Life in the Mafia* (New York: Signet, 1997), p. 104.

60   **What you have experienced:** Viktor E. Frankl, *Man's Search for Meaning,* revised and updated (New York: Pocket Books, 1997), p. 104.

61 **Me, John Gotti:** Jerry Capeci and Gene Mustain, *Gotti: Rise and Fall,* (New York: Onyx, 1996), p. 362.

62 **Never talk when:** Peter Elkind, *Rough Justice: The Rise and Fall of Eliot Spitzer* (New York: Portfolio, 2010), p. 8.

63 **"[Petrucelli] should kill":** United States v. Vittorio Amuso, 1992.

63 **Their way sure:** Joseph F. O'Brien and Andris Kurins, *Boss of Bosses: The Fall of the Godfather: The FBI and Paul Castellano* (New York: Island Books, 1991), p. 361.

64 **I felt terrible that:** Peter Maas, *Underboss: Sammy the Bull Gravano's Story of Life in the Mafia* (New York: HarperTorch, 1997), p. 132.

64 **Truman owes everything:** Sam Giancana and Chuck Giancana, *Double Cross: The Explosive, Inside Story of the Mobster Who Controlled America* (New York: Warner Books, 1992), p. 162.

67 **Maybe you didn't:** *Goodfellas,* DVD, screenplay by Nicholas Pileggi and Martin Scorsese, Winkler Films, 1990.

69 **"What the fuck's":** George Anastasia, *Blood and Honor: Inside the Scarfo Mob, the Mafia's Most Violent Family* (New York: William Morrow, 1991), p. 207.

69 **Don't start talking:** *The Sopranos,* "Down Neck," written by Robin Green and Mitchell Burgess, Season One, February 21, 1999.

70 **We have witnessed:** Stanley Milgram, *Obedience to Authority: An Experimental View* (New York: Harper Colophon Books, 1974), p. 123.

73 **He that is known:** Benjamin Franklin, *The Autobiography of Benjamin Franklin,* in *The Autobiography and Other Writings,* ed. L. Jesse Lemisch (New York: New American Library, 1985), p. 142.

74 **The marks of a true:** Paul Lunde, *Organized Crime: An Inside Guide to the World's Most Successful Industry* (London: DK, 2004), p. 57.

75 **[A]n ex-con named:** T. J. English, *Paddy Whacked: The Untold Story of the Irish American Gangster* (New York: Regan Books, 2005), p. 307.

78 **These investigations take:** Selwyn Raab, *Five Families: The Rise, Decline, and Resurgence of America's Most Powerful Mafia Empires* (New York: Thomas Dunne Books, 2005), p. 366.

79 **How poor are they:** William Shakespeare, *Othello,* in *The Riverside Shakespeare,* ed. G. Blakemore Evans (Boston: Houghton Mifflin Company, 1974), p. 1219.

80 **"That's what most":** Robert J. Schoenberg, *Mr. Capone: The Real—and Complete—Story of Al Capone* (New York: William Morrow & Co., 1992), p. 27.

81 **This system of ours:** Jerre Mangione and Ben Morreale, *La Storia: Five Centuries of the Italian Immigrant Experience* (New York: Harper Perennial, 1993), p. 259.

83 **Can everyone be:** Bryan Appleyard, "Can Everyone Be an Einstein?" *The Sunday Times* (London), November 16, 2008, Science, p. 23.

83 **Every saint has:** Oscar Wilde, *A Woman of No Importance,* in *The Importance of Being Earnest and Other Plays* (New York: Barnes & Noble Books, 2002), p. 144.

84 **I put men to death:** Leo Tolstoy, *My Confession* (London: Fount Paperbacks, 1995), p. 7.

85 **Cosa Nostra and:** "The Conglomerate of Crime," *Time,* August 22, 1969.

91 **Few men have any:** Ralph Waldo Emerson, *Representative Men,* ed. Pamela Schirmeister (New York: Marsilio Publishers, 1995), p. 156.

93 **The "Docile Don":** George Fresolone and Robert J. Wagman, *Blood Oath: The Heroic Story of a Gangster Turned Government Agent Who Brought Down One of America's Most Powerful Mob Families* (New York: Simon & Schuster, 1994), p. 54.

93 **At first, The Chin:** Philip Carlo, *Gaspipe: Confessions of a Mafia Boss* (New York: Harper, 2009), p. 183.

95 **Whatever happened in:** Peter Maas, *The Valachi Papers* (New York: Harper Paperbacks, 2003), p. 85.

96 **Organized crime is:** Paul Lunde, *Organized Crime: An Inside Guide to the World's Most Successful Industry* (London: DK, 2004), p. 8.

97 **In all illegal enterprises:** Hannah Arendt, *On Violence* (New York: Harcourt, Brace, Jovanovich, 1970), p. 67.

98 **That day, Tony and I:** Louis Ferrante, *Unlocked: The Life and Crimes of a Mafia Insider* (New York: Harper Paperbacks, 2009), p. 120.

100 **"We'll get some scuba":** Gene Mustain and Jerry Capeci, *Murder Machine: A True Story of Murder, Madness, and the Mafia* (New York: Onyx, 1993), p. 254.

105 **"Since ya like to":** John H. Davis, *Mafia Kingfish: Carlos Marcello and the Assassination of John F. Kennedy* (New York: Signet, 1989), p. 58.

106 **[Hymie] Weiss, notably:** Robert J. Schoenberg, *Mr. Capone: The Real—and Complete—Story of Al Capone* (New York: William Morrow & Co., 1992), p. 117.

107 **A Man of Honour can be:** From *Mafia Wars: The Confessions of Tommaso Buscetta,* by Tim Shawcross and Martin Young, in *The Mammoth Book of the Mafia,* eds. Nigel and Colin Cawthorne (Philadelphia: Running Press, 2009), p. 299.

108 **The wildest colts:** Plutarch, *The Lives of the Noble Grecians and Romans,* trans. John Dryden, rev. Arthur Hugh Clough (New York: The Modern Library, 1950), p. 134.

111 **"Japanese crime syndicates":** Louis Freeh and Howard Means, *My FBI: Bringing Down the Mafia, Investigating Bill Clinton, and Fighting the War on Terror* (New York: St. Martin's Press, 2005), p. 195.

112 **It's no surprise:** Philip Pullella, "Italy Seizes $1.9 Billion of Assets as Mafia Goes Green," Reuters, September 14, 2010.

113 **Other mobsters didn't seem:** T. J. English, *Paddy Whacked: The Untold Story of the Irish American Gangster* (New York: Regan Books, 2005), p. 184.

114 **The traditional mafioso:** Pino Arlacchi, *Mafia Business: The Mafia Ethic and the Spirit of Capitalism,* trans. Martin Ryle (London: Verso, 1987), p. 118.

116 **It's chiefly to my:** Ron Chernow, *Titan: The Life of John D. Rockefeller, Sr.* (New York: Random House, 1998), p. 223.

119 **"Get Gallo!":** Selwyn Raab, *Five Families: The Rise, Decline, and Resurgence of America's Most Powerful Mafia Empires* (New York: Thomas Dunne Books, 2005), p. 199.

119 **"Get Yamamoto!":** Bill Yenne, *Aces High: The Heroic Saga of the Two Top-Scoring American Aces of World War II* (New York: The Berkley Group, 2009), p. 114.

119 **"They bore down":** Edwin P. Hoyt, *Yamamoto: The Man Who Planned Pearl Harbor* (New York: McGraw-Hill, 1990), pp. 246–47.

121 **Humphreys gets the job:** Sam Giancana and Chuck Giancana, *Double Cross: The Explosive, Inside Story of the Mobster Who Controlled America* (New York: Warner Books, 1992), p. 75.

122 **"A clever girl":** Jacques Barzun, *From Dawn to Decadence: 1500 to the Present: 500 Years of Western Cultural Life* (New York: HarperCollins, 2000), p. 85.

124 **Everyone I know in the:** Selwyn Raab, *Five Families: The Rise, Decline, and Resurgence of America's Most Powerful Mafia Empires* (New York: Thomas Dunne Books, 2005), p. xi.

126 **In February of:** William F. Roemer, Jr., *Accardo: The Genuine Godfather* (New York: Ivy Books, 1996), p. 136.

127 **"Who's next on the":** Tim Pat Coogan, *Eamon De Valera: The Man Who Was Ireland* (New York: HarperCollins, 1995), p. 78.

128 **The eye sees:** William Shakespeare, *Julius Caesar,* in *The Riverside Shakespeare,* ed. G. Blakemore Evans (Boston: Houghton Mifflin Company, 1974) p. 1107.

128 **The unexamined life:** Plato, *The Trial and Death of Socrates,* trans. Benjamin Jowett (New York: Heritage Press, 1963), p. 95.

130   **[Tony Bender] was pretty**: Martin A. Gosch and Richard Hammer, *The Last Testament of Lucky Luciano* (Boston: Little, Brown, and Company, 1975), p. 115.

133   **The tongue was given**: Simon Sebag Montefiore, *Stalin: The Court of the Red Tsar* (New York: Alfred A. Knopf, 2003), p. 347.

134   **A handshake from**: *Godfathers Collection: The True History of the Mafia,* Volume Two, DVD, A&E Home Video/The History Channel, 2004.

135   **No one had any**: Louis Ferrante, *Unlocked: The Life and Crimes of a Mafia Insider* (New York: Harper Paperbacks, 2009), p. 21.

137   **[N]ever give an**: G. Lacour-Gayet, *Talleyrand (1754–1838),* Vol. 2 (1799–1815) (Paris: Payot, 1930), p. 44.

139   **These settlers may**: Livy, *A History of Rome, Selection*s, trans. Moses Hadas and Joe P. Poe (New York: The Modern Library, 1962), p. 213.

139   **It's in the DNA**: *Godfathers Collection: The True History of the Mafia,* Volume One, DVD, A&E Home Video/The History Channel, 2004.

139   **"I wouldn't do that"**: Fred D. Pasley, *Al Capone: The Biography of a Self-Made Man* (Whitefish, MT: Kessinger Publishing, 2004), p. 91.

139   **[Gotti's] one of the**: Philip Carlo, *Gaspipe: Confessions of a Mafia Boss* (New York: Harper, 2009), p. 136.

146   **Mr. and Mrs. Santo Trafficante**: Scott M. Deitche, *The Silent Don: The Criminal Underworld of Santo Trafficante, Jr.* (Fort Lee, N.J.: Barricade Books, Inc., 2007), p. 114.

146   **I had a great**: Robert Lacey, *Little Man: Meyer Lansky and the Gangster Life* (Boston: Little, Brown, and Company, 1991), p. 38.

147   **Aspasia . . . what great art**: Plutarch, *Lives of the Noble Grecians and Romans*, trans. John Dryden, rev. Arthur Hugh Clough (New York: The Modern Library, 1950), p. 200.

148   **"shattered a small"**: Otto Friedrich, *City of Nets: A Portrait of Hollywood in the 1940's* (Berkeley, CA: University of California Press, 1997), p. 265.

151   **[A don] must**: John H. Davis, *Mafia Dynasty: The Rise and Fall of the Gambino Crime Family* (New York: HarperTorch, 1994), p. 296.

153   **Human strength**: Ralph Waldo Emerson, *Representative Men,* ed. Pamela Schirmeister (New York: Marsilio Publishers, 1995), p. 106.

154   **[Don Angelo] Bruno wielded**: George Anastasia, *Blood and Honor: Inside the Scarfo Mob, the Mafia's Most Violent Family* (New York: William Morrow, 1991), p. 100.

154   **I'll have to hand**: Walter Noble Burns, *One Way Ride: The Red Trail of Chicago Gangland from Prohibition to Jake Lingle* (New York: Doubleday, Doran, 1931), p. 33.

155   **Sir, if there is one**: Peter Green, *Alexander of Macedon, 356–323 B.C.: A Historical Biography* (Berkeley: University of California Press, 1991), p. 410.

156   **Vito [Genovese] told me**: Martin A. Gosch and Richard Hammer, *The Last Testament of Lucky Luciano* (Boston: Little, Brown, and Company, 1975), p. 127.

157   **God deliver us**: Carlo D'Este, *Eisenhower: A Soldier's Life* (New York: Henry Holt and Company, 2002), p. 594.

160   **He plays politics**: William L. Riordan, *Plunkitt of Tammany Hall: A Series of Very Plain Talks on Very Practical Politics* (New York: Signet Classics, 1995), p. 55.

166   **Activities of the criminal**: Paul Lunde, *Organized Crime: An Inside Guide to the World's Most Successful Industry* (London: DK, 2004), p. 8.

167   **Senator Tobey: "You must"**: Kefauver Hearing, March 19, 1951.

169   **"Don't worry about"**: George Anastasia, *Blood and Honor: Inside the Scarfo Mob, the Mafia's Most Violent Family* (New York: William Morrow, 1991), p. 89.

170   **Wishful thinking is:** Steve Adubato, *What Were They Thinking?: Crisis Communication—The Good, the Bad, and the Totally Clueless* (Piscataway, N.J.: Rutgers University Press, 2008), p. 235.

171   **Perseus fell upon:** Livy, *A History of Rome, Selections,* Book 40, 182–179 B.C., trans. Moses Hadas and Joe P. Poe (New York: The Modern Library, 1962), p. 383.

173   **A table at:** Alex Witchel, "A Table at Rao's? Forgetaboutit," *New York Times,* February 14, 1996.

174   **They don't let you:** Selwyn Raab, *Five Families: The Rise, Decline, and Resurgence of America's Most Powerful Mafia Empires* (New York: Thomas Dunne Books, 2005), p. 199.

175   **We got Jews:** Jonathan Kwitny, *Vicious Circles: The Mafia in the Marketplace* (New York: W. W. Norton & Company, 1979), p. 66.

176   **I think [mobsters are]:** Peter Maas, *Underboss: Sammy the Bull Gravano's Story of Life in the Mafia* (New York: HarperTorch, 1997), p. 134.

177   **The women became:** Roberto Saviano, *Gomorrah:A Personal Journey into the Violent International Empire of Naples' Organized Crime System,* trans. Virginia Jewiss (New York: Picador, 2008), p. 144.

177   **"I don't interfere":** Richard West, *Tito and the Rise and Fall of Yugoslavia* (New York: Carroll & Graf Publishers, Inc., 1996), p. 330.

178   **His character and manners:** Plutarch, *Lives of the Noble Grecians and Romans,* trans. John Dryden, rev. Arthur Hugh Clough (New York: The Modern Library, 1950), p. 11.

178   **"I've barely been":** Clare Longrigg, *Boss of Bosses: A Journey into the Heart of the Sicilian Mafia* (New York: Thomas Dunne Books, 2008), p. 177.

178   **"We've been his":** Ibid.

180   **One thing Santo:** Frank Ragano and Selwyn Raab, *Mob Lawyer: Including the Inside Account of Who Killed Jimmy Hoffa and JFK* (New York: Charles Scribner's Sons, 1994), p. 218.

181   **When a mobster died:** Ibid., p. 294.

182   **[Capone] says we:** Carl Sifakis, *The Mafia Encyclopedia: From Accardo to Zwillman,* Third Edition (New York: Checkmark Books, 2005), p. 94.

183   **Many a poor family:** Robert J. Schoenberg, *Mr. Capone: The Real—and Complete—Story of Al Capone* (New York: William Morrow & Co., 1992), p. 292.

185   **After business, Carlos:** John H. Davis, *Mafia Kingfish: Carlos Marcello and the Assassination of John F. Kennedy* (New York: Signet, 1989), p. 66.

185   **"aloft in order to . . .":** Ross King, *Brunelleschi's Dome: How a Renaissance Genius Reinvented Architecture* (New York: Walker Publishing Co., 2000), p. 51.

185   **[Tony] Bananas always hosted:** George Fresolone and Robert J. Wagman, *Blood Oath: The Heroic Story of a Gangster Turned Government Agent Who Brought Down One of America's Most Powerful Mob Families* (New York: Simon & Schuster, 1994), p. 59.

188   **"[Napoleon's] presence on":** Robin Neillands, *Wellington and Napoleon: A Clash of Arms* (New York: Sterling Pub., 2002), p. 45.

188   **"The real reason":** Christopher Hibbert, *Wellington: A Personal History* (Reading, MA: Perseus Books, 1997), p. 14.

190   **Joe had a genius:** Gus Russo, *The Outfit: The Role of Chicago's Underworld in the Shaping of Modern America* (New York: Bloomsbury, 2001), p. 366.

196   **This is Joey:** Anthony M. DeStefano, *The Last Godfather: Joseph Massino and the Fall of the Bonanno Crime Family* (New York: Citadel Press, 2006), p. 168.

197   **"There's plenty for":** Robert J. Schoenberg, *Mr. Capone: The Real—and Complete—Story of Al Capone* (New York: William Morrow & Co., 1992), p. 24.

198   **"The essence of racketeering"**: Michael Riley, "A new tack Against Wal-Mart," *Denver Post*, September 6, 2004, p. C-01.

199   **The logic of criminal**: Roberto Saviano, *Gomorrah: A Personal Journey into the Violent International Empire of Naples' Organized Crime System*, trans. Virginia Jewiss (New York: Picador, 2008), p. 113.

207   **He will always be**: J. K. Hoyt, *The Cyclopedia of Practical Quotations: English, Latin & Modern Foreign Languages,* A New Edition, revised, corrected and enlarged (New York: Funk and Wagnall's, 1896), p. 705.

208   **The most successful CEOs**: David Prosser, "The Dizzy Heights," *The Independent* (London), June 15, 2010, p. 10.

210   **My father always said**: John Gotti, Jr., *60 Minutes* interview with Steve Kroft, April 11, 2010.

211   **Colombo had to go**: Joey Black and David Fisher, *Joey the Hitman: The Autobiography of a Mafia Killer* (New York: Thunder's Mouth Press, 2002), p. 201.

211   **I liked running booze**: T. J. English, *Paddy Whacked: The Untold Story of the Irish American Gangster* (New York: Regan Books, 2005), p. 144.

216   **[Provenzano] was worried**: Clare Longrigg, *Boss of Bosses: A Journey into the Heart of the Sicilian Mafia* (New York: Thomas Dunne Books, 2008), p. 208.

216   **I started learning about guns**: Albert DeMeo and Mary Jane Ross, *For the Sins of My Father: A Mafia Killer, His Son, and the Legacy of a Mob Life* (New York: Broadway Books, 2003), pp. 51–52.

217   **I rule with**: Clare Longrigg, *Boss of Bosses: A Journey into the Heart of the Sicilian Mafia* (New York: Thomas Dunne Books, 2008), p. 178.

218   **"I am Fuhrer"**: John Toland, *Adolf Hitler: The Definitive Biography* (New York: Anchor Books, 1992), p. 693.

219   **"This is gonna be"**: Michael Woodiwiss, *Organized Crime and American Power: A History* (Canada: University of Toronto Press, 2001), p. 287.

219   **"We have the *finest*"**: Kenneth Lay e-mail to Enron employees, August 8, 2001, "The Enron Investigation: Key Documents," *Washington Post Online*.

219   **The pride of your heart**: *Archaeologcal Study Bible: An Illustrated Walk Through Biblical History and Culture,* ed. Walter C. Kaiser, Jr., and Duane Garrett (Grand Rapids, Mich.: Zondervan Press, 2005), p. 1278.

221   **"by force and by fraud"**: Niccolo Machiavelli, *The Discourses,* ed. Bernard Crick, trans. Leslie J. Walker, S.J., rev. Brian Richardson (New York: Penguin Books, 1978), p. 310.

222   **"When the immortal"**: Julius Caesar, *The Gallic Wars and the Civil War,* trans. John Worrington (London: Heron Books, 1970), p. 7.

222   **Virtue's a thing that**: Plutarch, *Lives of the Noble Grecians and Romans,* trans. John Dryden, rev. Arthur Hugh Clough (New York: The Modern Library, 1950), p. 98.

BIBLIOGRAPHY

BOOKS

Adubato, Steve. *What Were They Thinking?: Crisis Communication—The Good, the Bad, and the Totally Clueless.* Piscataway, N.J.: Rutgers University Press, 2008.

Anastasia, George. *Blood and Honor: Inside the Scarfo Mob, the Mafia's Most Violent Family.* New York: William Morrow, 1991.

Archaeological Study Bible: An Illustrated Walk Through Biblical History and Culture. Edited by Walter C. Kaiser, Jr., and Duane Garrett. Grand Rapids, Mich.: Zondervan Press, 2005.

Arendt, Hannah. *On Violence.* New York: Harcourt, Brace, Jovanovich, 1970.

Aristophanes. *Aristophanes: The Complete Plays.* Translated by Paul Roche. New York: New American Library, 2005.

Arlacchi, Pino. *Mafia Business: The Mafia Ethic and the Spirit of Capitalism.* Translated by Martin Ryle. London: Verso, 1987.

Asada, Sadao. *From Mahan to Pearl Harbor: The Imperial Japanese Navy and the United States.* Annapolis, MD: Naval Institute Press, 2006.

Aurelius, Marcus. *Meditations.* Translated by Maxwell Staniforth. London: The Folio Society, 2003.

Barzun, Jacques. *From Dawn to Decadence: 1500 to the Present: 500 Years of Western Cultural Life.* New York: HarperCollins, 2000.

Beaumarchais, Pierre de. *The Marriage of Figaro.* Translated by John Wood. New York: Penguin Books, 2004.

Black, Joey, and David Fischer. *Joey the Hit Man: The Autobiography of a Mafia Killer.* New York: Thunder's Mouth Press, 2002.

Bonanno, Joseph, and Sergio Lalli. *A Man of Honor: The Autobiography of Joseph Bonanno.* New York: St. Martin's Paperbacks, 1983.

Bourrienne, Louis Antoine Fauvelet de. *Memoirs of Napoleon Bonaparte.* New and Revised Edition. Edited by R. W. Phipps. Volume 1. New York: Charles Scribner's Sons, 1891.

Brands, H.W. *The Age of Gold: The California Gold Rush and the New American Dream.* New York: Doubleday, 2002.

Bullock, Alan. *Hitler: A Study in Tyranny.* New York: Konecky and Konecky, 1962.

Bibliography

Burns, Walter Noble. *The One Way Ride: The Red Trail of Chicago Gangland from Prohibition to Jake Lingle*. New York: Doubleday, Doran, 1931.

Caesar, Julius. *The Gallic Wars and the Civil War*. Translated by John Worrington. London: Heron Books, 1970.

Capeci, Jerry, and Gene Mustain. *Gotti: Rise and Fall*. New York: Onyx, 1996.

Carlo, Philip. *Gaspipe: Confessions of a Mafia Boss*. New York: Harper, 2009.

———. *The Ice Man: Confessions of a Mafia Contract Killer*. New York: St. Martin's Press, 2006.

Chernow, Ron. *Titan: The Life of John D. Rockefeller, Sr*. New York: Random House, 1998.

Colvin, Geoff. *Talent Is Overrated: What Really Separates World-Class Performers from Everybody Else*. New York: Portfolio, 2008.

Confucius. *Confucius Analects, with Selections from Traditional Commentaries*. Translated by Edward Slingerland. Indianapolis, IN: Hackett Publishing Company, 2003.

Coogan, Tim Pat. *Eamon de Valera: The Man Who Was Ireland*. New York: HarperCollins, 1995.

Dallek, Robert. *Nixon and Kissinger: Partners in Power*. New York: HarperCollins, 2007.

Danziger, Danny, and John Gillingham. *1215: The Year of Magna Carta*. New York: Touchstone Books, 2004.

Davis, John H. *Mafia Dynasty: The Rise and Fall of the Gambino Crime Family*. New York: HarperTorch, 1994.

———. *Mafia Kingfish: Carlos Marcello and the Assassination of John F. Kennedy*. New York: Signet, 1989.

Deitche, Scott M. *The Silent Don: The Criminal Underworld of Santo Trafficante, Jr*. Fort Lee, NJ: Barricade Books, Inc., 2007.

DeMeo, Albert, and Mary Jane Ross. *For the Sins of My Father: A Mafia Killer, His Son, and the Legacy of a Mob Life*. New York: Broadway Books, 2003.

DeMille, Nelson. *The Gold Coast*. New York: Warner Books, 2006.

D'Este, Carlo. *Eisenhower: A Soldier's Life*. New York: Henry Holt and Company, 2002.

DeStefano, Anthony M. *The Last Godfather: Joseph Massino and the Fall of the Bonanno Crime Family*. New York: Citadel Press, 2006.

Eisenberg, Dennis, Uri Dan, and Eli Landau. *Meyer Lansky: Mogul of the Mob*. New York: Paddington Press, 1979.

Elkind, Peter. *Rough Justice: The Rise and Fall of Eliot Spitzer*. New York: Portfolio, 2010.

Ellis, Walter M. *Alcibiades*. London: Routledge, 1989.

Emerson, Ralph Waldo. *Representative Men*. Edited by Pamela Schirmeister. New York: Marsilio Publishers, 1995.

English, T. J. *Paddy Whacked: The Untold Story of the Irish American Gangster*. New York: Regan Books, 2005.

Ferrante, Louis. *Unlocked: The Life and Crimes of a Mafia Insider*. New York: Harper Paperbacks, 2009.

Fiandaca, Giovanni. *Women and the Mafia: Female Roles in Organized Crime Structures*. New York: Springer, 2007.

Fitzgerald, F. Scott. *The Great Gatsby*. New York: Scribner Paperback Fiction, 1995.

Flexner, James Thomas. *Washington: The Indispensable Man*. Boston: Little, Brown, and Company, 1974.

Follain, John. *The Last Godfathers: Inside the Mafia's Most Infamous Family*. New York: Thomas Dunne Books, 2009.

Frankl, Viktor E. *Man's Search for Meaning*, revised and updated. New York: Pocket Books, 1997.

Franklin, Benjamin. *The Autobiography and Other Writings*. Edited by L. Jesse Lemisch. New York: New American Library, 1985.

Fraser, Antonia. *Cromwell: Our Chief of Men*. London: Weidenfeld and Nicolson, 1973.

Freeh, Louis, and Howard Means. *My FBI: Bringing Down the Mafia, Investigating Bill Clinton, and Fighting the War on Terror*. New York: St. Martin's Press, 2005.

Fresolone, George, and Robert J. Wagman. *Blood Oath: The Heroic Story of a Gangster Turned Government Agent Who Brought Down One of America's Most Powerful Mob Families*. New York: Simon & Schuster, 1994.

Freud, Sigmund. *Beyond the Pleasure Principle*. Seattle, WA: Pacific Publishing Studio, 2010.

Friedrich, Otto. *City of Nets: A Portrait of Hollywood in the 1940's*. Berkeley: University of California Press, 1997.

Gentry, Curt. *J. Edgar Hoover: The Man and the Secrets*. New York: Plume, 1992.

Giancana, Sam, and Chuck Giancana. *Double Cross: The Explosive, Inside Story of the Mobster Who Controlled America*. New York: Warner Books, 1992.

Goldsworthy, Adrian. *Caesar: Life of a Colossus*. New Haven, CT: Yale University Press, 2006.

Gosch, Martin A., and Richard Hammer. *The Last Testament of Lucky Luciano*. Boston: Little, Brown, and Company, 1975.

Green, Peter. *Alexander of Macedon, 356–323 B.C.: A Historical Biography*. Berkeley: University of California Press, 1991.

Herodotus. *The Histories*. Revised Edition. Translated by Aubrey de Selincourt. New York: Penguin Books, 2003.

Hibbert, Christopher. *The House of Medici: Its Rise and Fall*. New York: Morrow Quill Paperbacks, 1980.

_____. *Wellington: A Personal History*. Reading, MA: Perseus Books, 1997.

Hoyt, Edwin P. *Yamamoto: The Man Who Planned Pearl Harbor*. New York: McGraw-Hill, 1990.

Hoyt, J. K. *The Cyclopedia of Practical Quotations: English, Latin & Modern Foreign Languages*. A New Edition, revised, corrected and enlarged. New York: Funk and Wagnalls, 1896.

Khrushchev, Nikita. *Khrushchev Remembers*. Translated and edited by Strobe Talbott. Boston: Little, Brown, 1970.

King, Ross. *Brunelleschi's Dome: How a Renaissance Genius Reinvented Architecture*. New York: Walker Publishing Co., 2000.

Kwitny, Jonathan. *Vicious Circles: The Mafia in the Marketplace*. New York: W. W. Norton & Company, 1979.

Lacey, Robert. *Little Man: Meyer Lansky and the Gangster Life*. Boston: Little, Brown, and Company, 1991.

Lacour-Gayet, G. *Talleyrand (1754–1838),* Vol. 2 (1799–1815). Paris: Payot, 1930.

Larsen, Lawrence H., and Nancy J. Hulston. *Pendergast!* Columbia: University of Missouri Press, 1997.

Livy. *A History of Rome, Selections.* Translated by Moses Hadas and Joe P. Poe. New York: The Modern Library, 1962.

Longrigg, Clare. *Boss of Bosses: A Journey into the Heart of the Sicilian Mafia.* New York: Thomas Dunne Books, 2008.

Lunde, Paul. *Organized Crime: An Inside Guide to the World's Most Successful Industry.* London: DK, 2004.

Maas, Peter. *Underboss: Sammy the Bull Gravano's Story of Life in the Mafia.* New York: HarperTorch, 1997.

_____. *The Valachi Papers.* New York: Harper Paperbacks, 2003.

McCullough, David. *Truman.* New York: Simon & Schuster, 1992.

Machiavelli, Niccolo. *The Discourses.* Edited by Bernard Crick, translated by Leslie J. Walker, S. J., with revisions by Brian Richardson. New York: Penguin Books, 1978.

_____. *The Prince, with Selections from The Discourses.* Edited and translated by Daniel Donno. New York: Bantam Books, 1985.

Mammoth Book of the Mafia: First-Hand Accounts of Life Inside the Mob. Edited by Nigel Cawthorne and Colin Cawthorne. Philadelphia: Running Press, 2009.

Manchester, William. *American Caesar: Douglas MacArthur, 1880-1964.* Boston: Little, Brown, and Company, 1978.

Mangione, Jerre, and Ben Morreale. *La Storia : Five Centuries of the Italian Immigrant Experience.* New York: Harper Perennial, 1993.

Marek, George R. *Beethoven: Biography of a Genius.* New York: Funk and Wagnalls, 1969.

Milgram, Stanley. *Obedience to Authority: An Experimental View.* New York: Harper Colophon Books, 1974.

Montefiore, Simon Sebag. *Stalin: The Court of the Red Tsar.* New York: Alfred A. Knopf, 2003.

_____. *Young Stalin.* London: Phoenix, 2008.

Mustain, Gene, and Jerry Capeci. *Murder Machine: A True Story of Murder, Madness, and the Mafia.* New York: Onyx, 1993.

Neillands, Robin. *Wellington and Napoleon: A Clash of Arms.* New York: Sterling Pub., 2002.

O'Brien, Joseph F., and Andris Kurins. *Boss of Bosses: The Fall of the Godfather: The FBI and Paul Castellano.* New York: Island Books, 1991.

Pasley, Fred D. *Al Capone: The Biography of a Self-Made Man.* Whitefish, MT: Kessinger Publishing, 2004.

Pileggi, Nicholas. *Casino: Love and Honor in Las Vegas.* New York: Simon & Schuster, 1995.

_____ *Wise Guy: Life in a Mafia Family.* New York: Pocket Books, 1987.

Pistone, Joseph D., and Richard Woodley. *Donnie Brasco: My Undercover Life in the Mafia.* New York: Signet, 1997.

Plato. *The Trial and Death of Socrates.* Translated by Benjamin Jowett. New York: Heritage Press, 1963.

Bibliography

Plutarch. *The Lives of the Noble Grecians and Romans.* Translated by John Dryden. Revised by Arthur Hugh Clough. New York: The Modern Library, 1950.

Puzo, Mario. *The Godfather.* New York: G. P. Putman's Sons, 1969.

Raab, Selwyn. *Five Families: The Rise, Decline, and Resurgence of America's Most Powerful Mafia Empires.* New York: Thomas Dunne Books, 2005.

Ragano, Frank, and Selwyn Raab. *Mob Lawyer: Including the Inside Account of Who Killed Jimmy Hoffa and JFK.* New York: Charles Scribner's Sons, 1994.

Ridley, Jasper. *Mussolini: A Biography.* New York: St. Martin's Press, 1998.

Riordan, William L. *Plunkitt of Tammany Hall: A Series of Very Plain Talks on Very Practical Politics.* New York: Signet Classics, 1995.

Roemer, William F., Jr. *Accardo: The Genuine Godfather.* New York: Ivy Books, 1996.

Rudolph, Robert. *The Boys from New Jersey: How the Mob Beat the Feds.* New Brunswick, NJ: Rutgers University Press, 1995.

Russo, Gus. *The Outfit: The Role of Chicago's Underworld in the Shaping of Modern America.* New York: Bloomsbury, 2001.

Saggio, Frankie, and Fred Rosen. *Born to the Mob: The True-Life Story of the Only Man to Work for All Five of New York's Mafia Families.* New York: Thunder's Mouth Press, 2004.

Saviano, Roberto. *Gomorrah: A Personal Journey into the Violent International Empire of Naples' Organized Crime System.* Translated by Virginia Jewiss. New York: Picador, 2008.

Schoenberg, Robert J. *Mr. Capone: The Real—and Complete—Story of Al Capone.* New York: William Morrow & Co., 1992.

Shakespeare, William. *The Riverside Shakespeare.* Edited by G. Blakemore Evans. Boston: Houghton Mifflin Company, 1974.

Shirer, William L. *The Rise and Fall of the Third Reich: A History of Nazi Germany.* New York: MJF Books, 1988.

Sifakis, Carl. *The Mafia Encyclopedia: From Accardo to Zwillman,* Third Edition. New York: Checkmark Books, 2005.

Snow, Edgar. *Red Star over China: The Classic Account of the Birth of Chinese Communism.* First Revised and Enlarged Edition. New York: Grove Press, 1968.

Sophocles. *The Oedipus Cycle: Oedipus Rex, Oedipus at Colonna, and Antigone.* English versions by Dudley Fitts and Robert Fitzgerald. New York: Harcourt, Brace, Jovanovich Publishers, 1977.

Suetonius, Gaius Tranquillus. *The Twelve Caesars.* Translated by Robert Graves. London: The Folio Society, 2002.

Thomas, Antony. *Rhodes: The Race for Africa.* London: BBC Books, 1996.

Thompson, Hunter S. *Song of the Doomed: More Notes on the Death of the American Dream.* New York: Simon & Schuster, 2002.

Thucydides. *The Peloponnesian War.* Translated by Benjamin Jowett. New York: Bantam Books, 1960.

Toland, John. *Adolf Hitler: The Definitive Biography.* New York: Anchor Books, 1992.

Tolstoy, Leo. *My Confession.* London: Fount Paperbacks, 1995.

West, Richard. *Tito and the Rise and Fall of Yugoslavia.* New York: Carroll and Graf Publishers, Inc., 1996.

Bibliography

Wilde, Oscar. *The Importance of Being Earnest and Other Plays*. New York: Barnes & Noble Books, 2002.

Woodiwiss, Michael. *Organized Crime and American Power: A History*. Canada: University of Toronto Press, 2001.

Yallop, David A. *In God's Name: An Investigation into the Murder of Pope John Paul I*. Toronto: Bantam Books, 1984.

Yenne, Bill. *Aces High: The Heroic Saga of the Two Top-Scoring American Aces of World War II*. New York: Berkley Publishing Group, 2009.

ARTICLES, REPORTS, AND TRANSCRIPTS

Appleyard, Bryan. "Can Everyone Be an Einstein?" *The Sunday Times* (London), November 16, 2008, Science, p. 34.

Brown, Nick. "Maltese Stands by His Mob Faux Pas." *Queens Courier,* November 29, 2007.

"The Conglomerate of Crime." *Time,* August 22, 1969, p. 31.

"The Enron Investigation: Key Documents." *The Washington Post Online,* www .washingtonpost.com/wp-srv/business/daily/transcripts/enron_keydocuments.html.

Kefauver Committee Interim Report #2, February 28, 1951. U.S. Senate Special Committee to Investigate Organized Crime in Interstate Commerce.

La Sorte, Mike. "Defining Organized Crime," May 2006, www.americanmafia.com/ Feature_Articles_349.html.

McPhee, Michele. "Brasco's Long Wait. After 20 Years, Ex-Agent Applauds Mob Bust." *New York Daily News,* January 19, 2003.

Marzulli, John. "Colombo Boss Alphonse (Allie Boy) Persico Sentenced to Life in Prison for 1999 Hit." *New York Daily News*, February 27, 2009.

———. "He's a Jolly Goodfella: Queens Beep Honors a Reputed Mobster." *New York Daily News,* February 14, 2004.

Pileggi, Nicholas. "The Mafia Is Good for You." *Saturday Evening Post,* November 30, 1968, pp. 18–21.

Prosser, David. "The Dizzy Heights." *The Independent* (London), June 15, 2010, p. 10.

Pullella, Philip. "Italy Seizes $1.9 Billion of Assets as Mafia Goes Green." Reuters, September 14, 2010.

Raab, Selwyn. "Double Portrait of a Man on Trial Astounds Friends." *New York Times,* April 11, 1995.

Rashbaum, William K. "Company with Big City Contracts Is Tied to Mob Schemes in Affidavit." *New York Times,* July 2, 2008.

"Remarks Announcing Federal Initiatives Against Drug Trafficking and Organized Crime." Speech given by President Ronald Reagan, October 14, 1982, www.reagan .utexas.edu/archives/speeches/1982/101482c.htm.

Riley, Michael. "A New Tack against Wal-Mart." *Denver Post*, September 6, 2004, p. C-01.

Rowan, Roy. "The Fifty Biggest Mafia Bosses." *Fortune,* November 10, 1986, pp. 24–35.

United States Congress. Senate. Special Committee to Investigate Organized Crime in Interstate Commerce (Kefauver Committee Hearings), Volume: pt. 7, Frank Costello Testimony, March 19, 1951, www.archive.org/details/investigationofo07unit.

United States v. Vittorio Amuso. United States District Court, Eastern District of New York, 1992.

Witchel, Alex. "A Table at Rao's? Forgetaboutit," *New York Times*, February 14, 1996.

DOCUMENTARY FILMS AND TELEVISION SHOWS

Godfathers Collection: True History of the Mafia. Two Volumes. DVD. A & E Home Video/ The History Channel, 2004.

Gotti, John, Jr. *60 Minutes* interview with Steve Kroft, CBS News, April 11, 2010.

Mafia Empire. DVD. Mpi Home Video, 2006.

Mobsters: Roy Demeo. Produced by Greg Scott. Towers Production, Inc. The Biography Channel, 2009.

The Sopranos, "Down Neck" episode. Written by Robin Green and Mitchell Burgess. Directed by Lorraine Senna Ferrara. Season One. February 21, 1999.

MOTION PICTURE FILMS

Goodfellas. DVD. Written by Nicholas Pileggi and Martin Scorsese. Directed by Martin Scorsese. Winkler Films, 1990.

SOUND RECORDINGS

Sinatra, Frank. "That's Life." Recorded October 18, 1966. Written by Dean Kay and Kelly Gordon. *That's Life.* Reprise Records, 1966. Produced by Jimmy Bowen. Vinyl recording.

INDEX

Abadinsky, Howard, 36, 96
Accardo, Anthony "Joe Batters," 13, 42–43,
  126, 174
Accardo, Clarice, 174
Accetturo, Anthony "Tumac," 55
Africanus, Scipio, 114–15
Aiello, Joseph, 211
Alcibiades, 131
Alexander the Great, 117, 155
Ambition
  and confidence, 10
  controlling, 153–55
  cultivating, 80–81
Amuso, Vittorio "Little Vic," 63
Anastasia, Albert "The Mad Hatter,"
  153, 155
Anastasia, George, 154
Anselmi, Albert, 139
Antigone, 70
Antony, Mark, 42
Aristophanes, 68
Arlacchi, Pino, 2, 114
Artie the Hair-Do, 21–22
Aspasia, 147
Aurelius, Marcus, 215
Authority
  corporate bosses, rules for. See CEOs,
    Mafia lessons for
  defying orders, 69–70, 103–4, 138–39
  getting respect from, 63–65
  respect for, 63–65
Avellino, Salvatore, 35–36, 78–79

Bacchus, 148
Bad-mouthing boss, avoiding, 42–44
Balagula, Marat, 191–92
Baldwin, Alec, 62
Banana Republic, 193
Barnes, Leroy "Nicky," 168
Basinger, Kim, 62
Batista, Fulgencio, 189
Beethoven, 102
Benjamin, Frank, 75
Betrayal
  bad-mouthing boss, 42–43
  counting on yourself over, 47–48
  friends, caution about, 156–57
  and Gravano, 13–14, 21, 24, 124–25
Bilotti, Joe, 21–22
Bilotti, Tommy, 21, 170
Bisaccia, Robert "Bobby Cabert," 32–33,
  66–67
Black, Joey, 211
Body language, 132–33
Bonanno, Joe "Joe Bananas," 46, 55, 146,
  193–94
Bonaparte, Napoleon, xxiii, 133, 154, 188
Bonding, with subordinates, 97–98
Bonventre, Cesare, 142
Bosses, CEOs as. See CEOs, Mafia
  lessons for
Boxers, mobsters as former, 33–34
Brain, change, capability for, 82–84
Brunelleschi, 185
Brunetti, John "Johnny Parkway," 53–54

Index

Bruno, Angelo "Gentle Don," 43, 93, 154, 169–70
Brutus, 40, 128
Buffett, Warren, 10
Burke, Jesse, 23
Burke, Jimmy, 13, 23
Business opportunities
    ancillary businesses, recognizing, 165–66
    foresight, value of, 189–90
    limitations, recognizing, 212–14
    versus opinions, 199–201
    recognizing, 35–39, 165–66
    short-term achievements, importance of, 144–45
    simple ideas, considering, 99–102
    untapped profits, finding, 39
Button men, 31

Caesar, Augustus, 154–55
Caesar, Julius, 12, 40, 103–4, 222
Caligula, 56–57
Cannone, Stefano "Stevie Beef," 97
Capo, middle managers as. see Management, Mafia lessons for
Capone, Al "Scarface," 1, 35, 42, 126, 76–77, 81, 113, 139, 154, 167, 183, 197–98, 209, 211–12
Capone, Immacolata, 177
Caponigro, Anthony "Tony Bananas," 169–70, 185–86
Caramandi, Nicky "The Crow," 75
Carlo, Philip, 93
Carter, Jimmy, 4
Carter, Rosalynn, 181
Carthage, 15–16, 114–15
Cash reserves, 206
Casso, Anthony "Gaspipe," 14, 26, 40–41, 93, 123, 138
Castellammarese War, 130
Castellano, Paul, 21, 24, 26, 46, 88–89, 103–4, 125, 170, 180
Castro, Fidel, 189–90
Cato the Younger, 40
CEOs, Mafia lessons for
    ambition, controlling, 153–55
    business opportunities, recognizing, 165–66

buzz, caution about, 203–4
cash reserves, maintaining, 206
charitable giving, 180–83
consigliere, choosing, 202
contingency plans, making, 164
crisis management, 169–72
discrimination, avoiding, 175–77
feeding employees, 184–86
foresight, value of, 189–90
franchise, time for, 209
friends, caution about, 156–57
hands-on boss, 187–88
hospitality, appreciating, 178–79
hubris, beware of, 218–19
inflated ego, dangers of, 210–11
inside information, getting, 205
interruptions, value of, 162–63
limits, recognizing, 212–14
and nepotism, 215–17
network, power of, 173–75
open-door to employees, 160–61
opinions versus business opportunities, 199–201
and opponents, 191–99
opponents, identifying, 193–96
overhead, controlling, 158–59
public relations, 170–72
survivorship, importance of, 207–8
tax payments, making, 167–68
Cerone, Jackie, 175
Chaeronea, Battle of, 117
Change, personal power for, 82–84
Charitable giving, 180–83
Charles I, king of England, 210
Chertoff, Michael, 39
Chiodo, "Fat Pete," 82, 123
Churchill, Winston, 89–90
Cicero, Marcus Tullius, 42–43
Civil War, American, 106–7
Claudius, 56–57
Coffey, Joe, 53
Collins, Michael, 126–27
Colombo, Joe, 55, 194, 211
Colombo War, 101
Colvin, Geoff, 20
Commissions, pay by, 9–10
Commodus, 215

Index

Competition, information about, 205
Confidence
  and ambition, 10
  building in employees, 116–17
Conflict resolution
  crisis management, 169–72
  for employees, 30
  sit-downs, 93–95
Confucius, 222
Consigliere, 169, 202
Construction industry, and Mafia, 5–6, 36, 153
Conte, Patsy, 3
Contingency plans, 164
Coppa, Frank, 97
Corallo, Anthony "Tony Ducks," 78–79
Costello, Frank, 52–53, 130–31, 167, 182, 208
Coughlin, Mae, 175
Crassus, 214
Crisis management, 169–72
Criticism, in private, 110
Crowe, Russell, 215
Cutolo, William "Wild Bill," 113–14

Darius, king of Persia, 201
Davis, John H., 38, 151, 185
Debts
  paying, 11, 73
  paying taxes, 167–68
DeCicco, Frankie, 125, 172
Decision-making
  on-the-fence position, avoiding, 130–31
  versus no decision, 142–43
  on-the-spot actions, avoiding, 136–37, 203–4
  and taking action, 118–20
DeFede, Joseph "Little Joe," 20
Delasco, Anthony "Ham," 33
Dellacroce, Aniello "O'Neil," 82
De'Medici, Catherine, 122
DeMeo, Albert, 216
DeMeo, Roy, 10, 87–88
DeMille, Nelson, 54
Demolition business, 37
De Niro, Robert, 23, 139
DeStefano, Sam, 25

Determination, quitting, never, xxiii, 32–34, 59–60
De Valera, Eamon, 126–27
Devine, Michael, 40
Dewey, Thomas, 35
Diapoulas, Peter "The Greek," 118
DiBello, George "Fat George," 19, 180, 183
DiBono, Louis, 125–26
DiNorscio, Giacomo "Jackie," 48
Discrimination, avoiding, 175–77
Dogs, Philly, 36–37
Donovan, Ray, 4
Drug trafficking, 25–26, 103, 154, 181, 199, 200

Earnings, by commission, 9–10
Eastwood, Clint, 113
Eboli, Tommy, 33
Eisenhower, Dwight, 90
E-mail, caution about, 61–62
Employees, Mafia lessons for
  ambition, cultivating, 80–81
  bad-mouthing boss, avoiding, 42–44
  benign comments, caution about, 61–62
  and chain of command, 63–70
  changing your life, power for, 82–84
  commission, compensation by, 9–10
  conflict resolution, 30
  debts, paying, 11, 73
  defying orders, time for, 69–70
  determination, 32–34
  experience/School of Hard Knocks, 58–60
  favors, cycle of, 52–54
  greed, resisting, 25–27
  hard work versus luck, 49–51
  hiring tactics, 9–10
  information, use of, 71–72
  intelligence, concealing, 55–57
  memory, sharpening, 19–20
  mistakes, learning from, 58–60
  networking, 28–31
  office politics, avoiding, 21–22
  opportunity, recognizing, 35–39
  patience, cultivating, 78–79
  playing dumb, time for, 55–57
  principle, standing on, 11–12

Index

Employees, Mafia lessons for (cont.)
quitting, never, 32–33, 59–60
respect, getting for work, 63–65
self-reliance, 47–48
sexual taboos, 40–41
silence, time for, 21–22, 32, 43, 74–75
tipping your hand, avoiding, 74–75
trustworthiness, 5, 23–24
values, most important, 17–18
verbal skills, necessity of, 45–46
work, loving the job, 13–16
wrongdoing, admitting, 76–77
Enemies. *See* Opponents
English, T. J., 113, 211
Enron, 153, 219
Eppolito, Jimmy, 181–82
Ethnic/racial groups, discrimination,
avoiding, 175–77
Expenses, overhead, controlling, 158–59
Experience, in School of Hard Knocks,
58–60

Facebook, 31
Faking it, playing dumb, time for, 55–57
Farace, Gus, 63, 138, 156
Fava, Anthony, 40–41
Favors, Circle of, 52–54
Federici, Anthony "Tough Tony," 182
Fever, Frankie, 203–4
Filocomo, Robert "Monkey Man," 97
Firing employees, and rehiring, 107–8
Flashiness, avoiding, 113–15
Flexibility, getting job done, 121–22
Foreman, Leo, 25
Franchise, time for, 209
Franklin, Benjamin, 73
Freeh, Louis, 111
Fresolone, George, 93, 186
Freud, Sigmund, 186
Friendships
caution about, 156–57
enemies, making friends with, 105–6
hospitality, appreciating, 178–79
subordinates, bonding with, 97–98

Gaggi, Nino, 87–88, 99–101
Galante, Carmine, 25–26

Gallo, Joe, 171
Gallo, Joseph "Crazy Joe," 118–19, 174
Gallucio, Frank "Galluch," 76–77
Gambino, Carlo, 74, 131, 146, 153–55
Gandhi, Mahatma, 69
Garbage collection business, 35–36
Garment District, and Mafia, 80, 153
Gender discrimination, avoiding, 175–77
Genovese, Carmine, 11
Genovese, Vito, 52–53, 130–31
Giancana, Sam, 42–43, 47, 64, 121
Gibson, Mel, 62
Gigante, Vincent "The Chin," 14, 33,
52–53, 55–56, 93
Giuliani, Rudolph, 3, 35, 183
Gladiator, 215
Goethe, 101
Golden, Cherie, 87–88
Gonzales, Alberto, 62
Goodfellas, 19, 23, 67
Goombah, 32
Gotti, Gene, 103
Gotti, John, Jr., 183, 210
Gotti, John, Sr., 21–22, 61, 80–81, 103–4,
113, 124–25, 138–39, 154, 170–72, 219
Grasso, Pietro, 216
Gravano, Sammy "The Bull," 13–14, 21,
24, 64, 124–26, 176, 202
Graziano, Anthony, 196
Greco, Pino, 74–75
Greece, ancient, xix, xxiv, 70–71, 129,
147–48, 201–2, 218
Greed, resisting, 25–27
Grimaldi, Vito, 182
Guzik, Jake, 175

Hannibal, 15–16
Harvard Inn, 76
Hatcher, Everett, 63, 138
Hawking, Stephen, 91
Helfant, Edwin, 134–35
Henry II, king of France, 122
Henry IV, king of Germany, 108–9
Herodotus, 200–201
Hickok, Wild Bill, 113–14
Hill, Henry, 13
Hill, Virginia, 147–48

Index

Hiring
 after firing, 107–8
 commission-based compensation, 9–10
History, lessons from, 146–48, 154–55, 192,
  218, 221–22. *See also* Greece, ancient;
  Roman Empire; *individual historical
  figures*
Hitler, Adolf, 89–90, 218–19
Holocaust, 27
Hospitality
 appreciation for, 178–79
 feeding employees, 184–86
Hot-dog business, 26–27, 36–37
Howard, Joe, 175
Hubris, 218–19
Humphreys, Murray "The Camel," 7,
  121, 166

Ianniello, Matty "The Horse," 36
Information, value of, 71–72, 111–12, 205
Inside information, 205
Intelligence
 history, learning from, 146–48
 of mobsters, 1–2, 146
 playing dumb, time for, 55–57
 verbal skills, necessity of, 45–46
Interruptions, value of, 162–63
Inzerillo, Giuseppe, 74–75
Inzerillo, Salvatore, 74
Ireland, revolutionary movement, 126–27

James, Frank, 23
James, Jesse, 23
Jealousy, and playing dumb, 55–57
John, king of England, 210
John Paul I, Pope, 171
Johnson, Bumpy, 182
Jones, Jim, 181

Key Food, 3
Khruschchev, Nikita, 59
Kunstler, William, 48

Lansky, Meyer, 1, 19, 43, 105, 134, 146, 189
Las Vegas, 1, 146–47
Lay, Kenneth, 153, 219
Liberatore, Anthony, 116

Licatesi, Tony, 98
Lino, Frank, 97
Lino, Robert, Sr., 97
Linsey, James, 198
Lombardozzi, Carmine, 107–8
Loyalty
 bullet for boss, taking, 96
 caution about, 24
 to employees, 138–39
Luciano, Charles "Lucky," 18, 32, 49–51,
  105, 118, 130, 156, 175–76, 189
Luck, versus hard work, 49–51
Lunde, Paul, 74, 166
Luparelli, Joseph, 174
Lupo, Salvatore, 32

MacArthur, Douglas, 64
McGurn, Jack "Machine Gun," 33, 126
Machiavelli, 138, 146, 154, 171, 221–22
McLaughlin, Punchy, 82
Made members, 31
Madoff, Bernie, 26
Mafia
 American Founder of, 49–50
 bonding rituals, 97
 bosses, rules for. *See* CEOs, Mafia
  lessons for
 button men, 31
 consigliere, role of, 169, 202
 employees, rules for. *See* Employees,
  Mafia lessons for
 hits, reasons for, 25–26, 40, 42–43, 63,
  87–89, 104, 114, 125–26, 134–39,
  147–48, 181–82, 191–92, 195–96
 intelligence of, 1–2
 legit business success by, 1–6
 legit institutions similarity to,
  xxi–xxii, 27
 loving the work, 13–14
 made members, 31
 middle managers, rules for. *See*
  Management, Mafia lessons for
 nicknames, purpose of, 19–20
 non-Italians in, 175–77, 189
 parallel economy of, 38–39
 personality traits, 2, 33, 38
 Sinatra, admiration of, 32, 34

Index

Mafia (cont.)
  sit-downs, 93–95
  social clubs, 160, 186–87
  as social network, 30–31
  studying , reasons for, xix, xxii–xxiii, 4
  technology, knowledge of, 111–12
  women in, 176–77
Magliocco, Joseph, 194
Maltese, Serphin, 182
Management, Mafia lessons for
  action, taking, 118–20
  body language, understanding, 132–33
  bullet for boss, taking, 96
  confidence building by, 116–17
  conflict resolution, 93–95
  criticism, in private, 110
  decision-making, 118–20, 130–31,
    136–37, 142
  employees, loyalty to, 138–39
  enemies, making friends with, 105–6
  on-the-fence position, avoiding, 130–31
  firing and rehiring, 107–8
  flashiness, avoiding, 113–15
  flexibility and getting job done, 121–22
  goods, delivering, 134–35
  history, lessons from, 146–48
  leaving organization, 149–50
  mastermind as leader, 91–92
  motivating workers, 91–92
  real versus insignificant problems, 123
  relaxation, value of, 140–41
  respect from, 124–27
  self-analysis, 128–29
  short-term achievements, importance of,
    144–45
  simple ideas, considering, 99–102
  on-the-spot actions, avoiding, 136–37
  staff, bonding with, 97–98
  staff, responsibility for actions of, 87–90
  technology, knowledge of, 111–12
  ultimatums, dealing with, 103–4
Mao, Madame, 177
Maranzano, Salvatore, 11–12, 18, 95, 118,
  130, 175–76
Marcello, Carlos, 23, 38, 105–6, 144–45,
  175, 182
Maresca, Pupetta "Madame Camorra," 176

Marie Antoinette, 186
Marshall, Helen, 182
Martens, Frederick, 35, 37
Masseria, Joe "The Boss," 130
Massino, Joe, 13, 20, 88–89, 97, 194–96
Mastermind, as motivator, 91–92
Maxwell, John, 127
Mazza, Anna "The Black Widow," 176
Meatpacking industry, 26–27, 38–39
Memory, improving, 19–20
Merkel Meat, 26–27
Messineo, Francesco, 112
Milgram, Stanley, 70
Milito, Louie, 22
Mirra, Anthony, 89
Mistakes, learning from, 58–60
Mnemonics, 19–20
Mobsters. See Mafia
Montefiore, Simon Sebag, 59
Motivation of staff, by management, 91–92
Mouw, Bruce, 78
Murder, Inc., 153
Mussolini, Benito, 52, 142–43
Mussolini, Vittorio, 142–43
MySpace, 31

Napolitano, Dominick "Sonny Black," 14,
  88–89, 97, 140, 195–96
Nazis, 27, 89–90
Nepotism, 215–17
Networking
  elite group, power of, 173–75
  favors, cycle of, 52–54
  importance of, 28–31
Newton, Sir Isaac, 36
New York City, Mafia construction
  projects in, 5–6, 36
Nuremberg defense, 125

O'Banion, Dean, 211
Obinu, Mauro, 139
Office politics, avoiding, 21–22
Open-door policy, for employees, 160–61
Opponents
  alliance with, 105–6
  decisive action, taking, 118–20
  identifying, 193–96

Index

Mafia hits, reasons for, 25–26, 40, 42–43,
  63, 87–89, 104, 114, 125–26, 134–39,
  147–48, 181–82, 191–92, 195–96
 neutralizing, 197–98
 tipping your hand, avoiding, 74–75
 underestimating, avoiding, 191–92
Orbach, Jerry, 118
Orena, Victor "Little Vic," 187–88
Organized labor, 153
Overhead, controlling, 158–59

Parthenon, 147–48
Patience, cultivating, 78–79
Patton, George S., 157
Pearl Harbor, 119
Pellegrino, Frank "Frankie No," 173
Pendergast, Tom "Boss Tom," 24
Pendergast Machine, 24, 64
Penovich, Pete, 209
Pericles, 147–48
Persico, Alphonse "Allie Boy," 2, 112
Persico, Carmine "The Snake," 1-2, 47–48,
  140, 187–88
Petrizzo, Thomas, 4–5
Petrucelli, John, 63, 156
Philip II, king of Macedon, 117
Pileggi, Nicholas, 13, 20, 50
Piney, Joe, 172
Pistone, Joe, 59, 88–89, 196
Pizza Connection, 200
Plato, 71
Plutarch, 103
Pompey, 12
Porn industry, 18
Prince (Machiavelli), 221–22
Principle, standing on, 11–12
Privacy, versus interruptions, 162–63
Profaci, Salvatore, 5
Provenzano, Bernardo, 82, 178–79, 207–8,
  215–17
Public relations, 170–72
Pungitore, Joe, 69
Puzo, Mario, 53

Quinn, John, 87
Quitting, never quitting, xxiii, 32–34,
  59–60

Raab, Selwyn, 52, 124
Ragano, Frank, 180–81
Rao's, 173
Rastelli, Philip "Rusty," 194–95
Reagan, Ronald, 4
Relaxation, value of, 140–41
Resignation, leaving organization, 149–50
Respect
  for all employees, 124–27
  for chain of command, 63–65
  getting, 63–65
Responsibility
  for actions of staff, 87–90
  keeping secrets. *See* Trustworthiness
Revolutionary War, 50
Reznikov, Vladimir, 191–92
Riina, Giovanni, 216
Riina, Totò, 215–16
Riordan, William L., 160
Roman Empire, 11–12, 15–16, 40, 56–57,
  103, 114–15, 139, 154–55, 171, 214–15
Rosenberg, Chris, 10
Ruggiero, Angelo, 103, 138
Russian-American Mob, 191–92

Salerno, Anthony "Fat Tony," 46, 140
Salerno, Ralph, 134
Santa Claus business, 38
Santino, Umberto, 38
Saviano, Roberto, 177, 200
Scalise, John, 139
Scarfo, Nicodemo "Little Nicky,"
  43–44, 69
Scarpa, Gregory, Sr., 101
Schiller, Friedrich, 102
Schoenberg, Robert J., 80, 106
School of Hard Knocks, 58–60
Scialo, Carmine "Mimi," 74
Sciascia, Gerlando, 97, 195–96
Scotto, Anthony, 4
Self-analysis, 128–29
Self-reliance, 47–48
Serraino, Maria, 176–77
Seybert, Joanna, 2
Shawcross, Tim, 41, 107
Siegel, Benjamin "Bugsy," 1, 146–47, 189
Silence, time for, 21–22, 32, 43, 74–75